PEOPLE
—— *of the* ——
BLESSING

To Harriet, Jemima and Tabitha

Text copyright © James Jones 1991, 1998
The author asserts the moral right
to be identified as the author of this work

Published by
The Bible Reading Fellowship
Peter's Way, Sandy Lane West
Oxford OX4 5HG
ISBN 1 84101 053 7

First published 1991
Revised edition 1998
10 9 8 7 6 5 4 3 2 1 0

Acknowledgments
The *New Revised Standard Version* of the Bible, copyright © 1989 by the Division of
Christian Education of the National Council
of the Churches of Christ in the USA.
The *Revised Standard Version* of the Bible, copyright © 1971 and 1952 by the Division of
Christian Education of the National Council of the Churches of Christ in the USA.
The *New International Version*, copyright © 1973, 1978, 1984 by the International Bible
Society. Published by Hodder & Stoughton.
The Jerusalem Bible © 1966 by Darton, Longman & Todd Ltd and Doubleday and Co. Inc.
The Psalms: a new translation for worship © English text 1976, 1977 David L. Frost, John A.
Emerton, Andrew A. Macintosh, all rights reserved, © pointing William Collins Sons &
Co. Ltd.
Extracts from the Book of Common Prayer of 1662, the rights in which are invested in the
Crown in perpetuity within the United Kingdom, are reproduced by permission of the
Crown's patentee, Cambridge University Press.
'Safe in the shadow of the Lord' is copyright © Timothy Dudley-Smith. Used by
permission.
'I gave myself to Love Divine' by St Teresa of Avila, translated by E. Allison Peers. Used by
permission of Sheed & Ward Ltd.
'Gloria in Excelsis' as it appears in *The Alternative Service Book 1980* is copyright © 1970,
1971, 1975 International Consultation on Englsih Texts (ICET) and is reproduced by
permission.
'Hosanna to the Son of David' by Mavis Ford. Copyright © 1978 Word's Spirit of Praise
Music. Administered by Copycare, PO Box 77, Hailsham, BN27 3EF UK. Used by
permission.

A catalogue record for this book
is available from the British Library

Printed and bound in Great Britain by
Caledonian Book Manufacturing International, Glasgow

PEOPLE

—— *of the* ——

BLESSING

JAMES JONES

INTRODUCTION

I have always found it difficult to understand what 'blessing' means. 'Happiness' seems too flimsy a word: rather like carrying water in a paper bag, the word does not hold the full weight of the meaning of blessing.

The meaning of words emerges from the context in which we find them. The Book of Psalms gives us over thirty occasions when the word 'blessed' is used. It is associated with a range of experiences from 'blessed is the one who considers the poor' to 'blessed is the one whose sins are forgiven'; from 'blessed is the one whom the Lord disciplines' to 'blessed is the one who trusts in the Lord'. It is only when we consider all these experiences together that we begin to understand the full meaning of being blessed by God. Just as a rainbow is more than one colour so, too, being blessed by God consists of many strands.

Although this was originally published as a Lent book I have discovered that people have used it throughout the year. The possibility of being blessed by God has a timeless and universal appeal. In these pages I have concentrated on those psalms in which we find the promise of God's blessing. Each promise leads on to a reflection which, although not an exposition of the psalm, does, I hope, have integrity with the text. I then offer a corresponding word from Jesus and a prayer, poem or spiritual exercise that encourages us to enter into the experience of blessing. The book ends with a reflection on Psalm 22 because there are inevitably times when the experience of blessing seems very remote. Hopefully it will encourage you to journey on through the rest of the psalms in which you will find every mood and emotion.

I pray that in entering into these psalms your experience will be that of delighting in God who delights in us.

ACKNOWLEDGMENTS

It is good to see the psalms featuring more in worship and in books on spirituality. I have greatly appreciated Harry Mowvley's translation of the psalms (Collins, 1989). My colleague when I was at Christ Church, Clifton, the Musical Director Dr Berj Topalian, has been translating and setting the psalms to music for many years; his original musical and poetic interpretations of the psalms have been an inspiration to me as I have written this collection.

The direct translations of the psalms throughout this book are taken from the Revised Standard and New International Versions of the Bible and the Alternative Service Book. I have also used the Jerusalem Bible for Psalm 37 on page 28; Artur Weiser's translation of Psalm 112 on page 80 (*The Psalms*, Old Testament Library Series, SCM Press, 1979); and the Book of Common Prayer for Psalm 121 on page 107.

CONTENTS

In SEARCH
of BLESSING

GREEN TREES
and STREAMS *of* WATER

PSALM 1 : 1—6

Blessed is the man who has not walked in the counsel of the ungodly:
nor followed the way of sinners
nor taken his seat amongst the scornful.
But his delight is in the law of the Lord:
and on that law he will ponder day and night.
He is like a tree planted beside streams of water:
that yields its fruit in due season.
Its leaves also shall not wither:
and look whatever he does it shall prosper.

As for the ungodly, it is not so with them:
they are like the chaff which the wind scatters.
Therefore the ungodly shall not stand up at the judgment:
nor sinners in the congregation of the righteous.
For the Lord cares for the way of the righteous:
but the way of the ungodly shall perish.

The PROMISE *of* BLESSING

Blessed is the man who has not walked in the counsel of the ungodly:
nor followed the way of sinners
nor taken his seat amongst the scornful.
But his delight is in the law of the Lord:
and on that law he will ponder day and night.

A REFLECTION

When in a city and with time to spare between appointments I often escape into a church. As I have passed through the great doors on a humid summer's day I have left behind the noise and heat, the fumes and the jostling crowds and entered the cool serenity of another world. Just feet away the urban fever still rages but here in this sanctuary there is space for renewal.

This first psalm provides for us the great west door into the book of psalms and into the blessing promised to those who will sit and ponder on the law of the Lord. It presents us with two worlds: the world of bedlam and the world of sanity. There are two ways: the way of destruction and the way of righteousness.

Do we fail to see that two such worlds exist? Do we fail to see that there are attitudes and aspirations at large that conflict with those of God? If so, this means that we have reached one of two situations. Either, Christian values have so permeated our culture that society has been effectively Christianized and the divide bridged. Or, Christians are so conformed to, and moulded by, their contemporaries that they have lost their distinctive grit.

This psalm comes to us as a personal stirring of the conscience to resist deliberately the influences of those who have voted God out of office. Such influences are strong, persuasive and insidious.

John Newton, even after his dramatic conversion to the Lord Jesus Christ, continued to command a slave-ship. He studied the Bible while ferrying slaves across the Atlantic, and prayed in his cabin while, feet beneath him, men and women died in the suffocating and disease-ridden bowels of his ship. It took the Holy Spirit a few more years to shake his servant out of the moral numbness induced by 'the counsel of the ungodly'.

Of course, we find such behaviour hard to believe. How could a committed Christian do such a thing? The point is that we need to ask the spirit of truth to diagnose our own blind spots. What will future generations view with incredulity when they examine the relationship of today's Church with the world?

The positive step that is held before us to counteract the negative influences is to delight in God's word and to meditate on his truths. Delight suggests something unhurried. In our hectic schedules we do not often leave time for the leisurely and time-consuming art of delighting. People who delight in a view do not quickly glance at it: they linger, reflect, absorb, savour, appreciate, and enjoy what they see. Their delighting both expresses and nourishes their character.

This psalm gives us a picture of such a person. He or she is like 'a tree planted beside streams of water; that yields its fruit in due season'. Meditate on this. Dwell on this picture. Imagine the hidden roots of the tree searching out the life-giving water. Look into the crystal-clear water of the stream. Feel its cold vigour. Taste its earthy and vital purity. Let yourself crave for the refreshment of such cooling streams; let your thirst for renewal be quenched as you take time to meditate on the promise of this psalm.

A WORD *from* JESUS

Remember the words of Jesus:

> 'Let anyone who is thirsty come to me, and let the one who believes in me drink. As the scripture has said, "Out of the believer's heart shall flow rivers of living water."' Now he said this about the Spirit... (John 7:37–39)

A MEDITATION

Lord, I come.
Into the sanctuary of your presence I come.
Leaving behind for a while all the distractions of my daily life.
Lord, I come.

Lord, I come.
Sullied by compromise, flawed with self-centredness, soiled by sin.
Conscious that unconsciously I have absorbed
attitudes and values and aspirations
that are at odds with your unadulterated goodness,
your sheer beauty,
your healing purposes,
your compassionate justice.

Lord, I come.
Rid me of the sour taste of sin.
Lord, I come.
Wet my lips with the sweet taste of your word.
Cause me to savour every word,
glean every nuance,
cherish every sight of you.

Let the roots of my being go in search of you.
Let them be nourished by the cool waters of your Spirit.
Let your life renew my life.
Let your life satisfy.
Let your life be my blessing
And yield its fruit in due season.

TURMOIL & UNCERTAINTY

PSALM 2:1–11

Why are the nations in tumult:
and why do the peoples cherish a vain dream?
The kings of the earth rise up
and the rulers conspire together;
against the Lord and against his anointed saying,
'Let us break their bonds asunder:
let us throw off their chains from us.'

He that dwells in heaven shall laugh them to scorn:
the Lord will hold them in derision.
Then he will speak to them in his wrath
and terrify them in his fury:
'I the Lord have set up my king on Zion my holy hill.'

I will announce the Lord's decree
That which he has spoken:
'You are my son, this day I have begotten you.
Ask of me
and I will give you the nations for your inheritance:
the uttermost parts of the earth for your possession.
You shall break them with a rod of iron:
and shatter them in pieces like a potter's vessel.'

Now therefore be wise O kings:
be advised you that are judges of the earth.
Serve the Lord with awe
and govern yourselves in fear and trembling:
lest he be angry and you perish in your course.

The PROMISE *of* BLESSING

For his wrath is quickly kindled:
blessed are those that turn to him for refuge.

A REFLECTION

The events of the late 1980s were as surprising as a sudden storm. Nobody ever imagined we would see the dismantling of the Berlin Wall and the disintegration of communist governments in Eastern Europe. It was unpredictable, and as relentless as an incoming tide. Even those hardline governments which seemed like castles set in concrete yielded and collapsed like sandcastles under the rising tide of populism. Yet on these beaches is now to be found the flotsam of uncertainty. There are the simmering tensions in Russia and the new republics, economic hardship in countries such as Albania, and the ongoing anguish of much of the former Yugoslavia. The nations of the world are still 'in tumult'.

It was in a similar situation of political and social upheaval that this psalm was written. In between the death of one king and the anointing of another there were often popular uprisings. Every change in government is marked by a degree of turmoil and uncertainty. This scenario provides the canvas on which the psalmist paints a picture of contrast between the political ambitions of people and the purposes of God.

The psalm was actually sung at the coronation of a new king. The first three verses speak about the kings of the earth and their political aspirations and strategies; the second set of verses is about the heavenly king who rules over the world; the third section imagines an ideal king who will rule a rebellious world with a rod of iron.

It is not difficult to see how the Jews, constantly disappointed by rulers who failed them and continually frustrated by the oppressive rulers of foreign powers, began to look forward to an 'anointed one' (this is the meaning of the word 'messiah', Hebrew in origin, and 'Christ', Greek in origin). The Lord's anointed would fulfil their aspirations for a kingdom of justice and peace.

The followers of Jesus began to see that Jesus himself was the Lord's anointed—the messiah or Christ—the one who would usher in God's Kingdom. That is why this psalm features so often in the New Testament about Jesus (see Matthew 3:17; 17:5; Acts 13:33; Hebrews 1:5; 5:5). When Jesus stood in front of Pilate at his trial, he recognized two things that are explicit in this psalm and important to note. Firstly, he said, 'My kingdom is not from this world' (John 18:36). This does not mean that Jesus' kingdom has nothing to do with this world. The words mean: 'My kingship does not derive from men and women.' It is God who designates and anoints Jesus as King (see Psalm 2:5–7). And although the kingship of Jesus does not derive from human election his kingdom is, without doubt, expected to extend to and touch every corner of the earth. Secondly, Jesus informs Pilate: 'You would have no power over me unless it had been given you from above' (John 19:11). Jesus recognized the ultimate sovereignty of God over all human affairs (see Psalm 2:4). God is in control even though at times the course of events takes an unpredictable or even bizarre turn.

Because power corrupts and absolute power corrupts absolutely, it is life-saving that those in power (in the world, society, companies, unions, households, local communities) remember the warning of Jesus to Pilate that they are accountable in the end to God. 'Serve the Lord with awe and govern yourselves in fear and trembling' (Psalm 2:10). As we rejoice at the ending of harsh dictatorships we must pray that they do not give rise to a different form of godless oppression: 'For his wrath is quickly kindled: blessed are those that turn to him for refuge' (Psalm 2:11).

A WORD *from* JESUS

At his baptism there was,

> *A voice from heaven saying: 'This is my Son, the Beloved, with whom I am well pleased'* (Matthew 3:17).

At his transfiguration,

> *A voice from the cloud said: 'This is my Son, the Beloved; with him I am well pleased'* (Matthew 17:5).

There was no such comforting voice from heaven when Jesus died alone upon the cross. Yet because of his passion and death we may now hear the Lord of heaven and earth say to each of us: 'This is my beloved child, with whom I am well pleased.'

A PRAYER

Lay before you the world news of a daily newspaper. Read each of the stories' headlines, then praise God.

> *Blessed be the name of God from age to age,*
> *for wisdom and power are his.*
> *He changes times and seasons,*
> *deposes kings and sets up kings;*
> *he gives wisdom to the wise*
> *and knowledge to those who have understanding.*
> *He reveals deep and hidden things;*
> *he knows what is in the darkness,*
> *and light dwells with him. (Daniel 2:20–22)*

PORTRAIT *of* PERFECTION

PSALM 24:1–10

The earth is the Lord's and the fullness thereof,
the world and those who dwell therein;
for he has founded it upon the seas,
and established it upon the rivers.

Who shall ascend the hill of the Lord?
And who shall stand in his holy place?
He who has clean hands and a pure heart,
who does not lift up his soul to what is false,
and does not swear deceitfully.
He will receive blessing from the Lord,
and vindication from the God of his salvation.
Such is the generation of those who seek him,
who seek the face of the God of Jacob.

Lift up your heads, O gates!
and be lifted up, O ancient doors!
that the King of glory may come in.
Who is the King of glory?
The Lord, strong and mighty,
the Lord, mighty in battle!
Lift up your heads, O gates!
and be lifted up, O ancient doors!
that the King of glory may come in.
Who is this King of glory?
The Lord of hosts,
he is the King of glory!

The PROMISE *of* BLESSING

He will receive blessing from the Lord,
and vindication from the God of his salvation.

A REFLECTION

This is a psalm about entering into the worship of God. The verse which precedes the promise of blessing is daunting for any with an awareness of the dark side of their nature:

> *He who has clean hands and a pure heart,*
> *who does not lift up his soul to what is false,*
> *and does not swear deceitfully.*

Here is a portrait of perfection that tells the aspiring worshipper who is flawed by sin that there is no space for the likes of him in the 'holy place'! Who on earth has clean hands, a pure heart, never lies nor breaks a promise? It has been said that if we could devise a camera to photograph our thoughts then none of us would have a friend in the world! Many of us are grateful that our heart is not worn on our sleeve and that, for the most part, it remains well hidden. Yet it is God who knows our hearts and nothing can be hidden from him.

Purity for the Jewish worshippers was secured by the high priest entering the Holy Place in the temple and offering a sacrifice on behalf of the people. The sacrifice was an effective prayer that both sought and assured them of the forgiveness of God. Now through the sacrificial death of Jesus, God forgives us uniquely and eternally. 'And every priest stands day after day at his service, offering again and again the same sacrifices that can never take away sins. But when Christ had offered for all time a single sacrifice for sins, 'he sat down at the right hand of God'... and the Holy Spirit also testifies to us... "I will remember their sins and their lawless deeds no more"... Therefore, my friends, since we have confidence to enter the sanctuary by the blood of Jesus... let us approach with a true heart in full assurance of faith, with our hearts sprinkled clean from an evil conscience and our bodies washed with pure water' (Hebrews 10:11, 12, 15, 17, 19, 22). Through Jesus we can find clean hands and a pure heart and enter fully into the worship of God.

This psalm also speaks about the gates of the temple being opened to the King of Glory and imagines God taking his place upon his throne, the ark, at the heart of the temple.

The Christian believer is encouraged to see himself and the Christian community as the new temple in which the Lord by his Spirit resides (see 1 Corinthians 6:19, 20 and 2 Corinthians 6:16–18). This truth is often captured in the image of us asking the risen Christ to enter our hearts. But this sort of language and imagery can sometimes be misleading, especially for children with whom it is most often used.

A few years ago, when my three teenage daughters were much younger, I remember one day when they were jumping all over me as I was lying on the floor. When I protested at yet another blow to my solar plexus, 'Please, don't jump on Daddy's tummy,' one of my daughters piped up in my defence, 'No, or you'll squash Jesus!' But, although such talk about asking Jesus into our hearts can lead to misunderstanding, it does reflect a biblical spirituality that ought not to be neglected.

The apostle Paul, writing to the factious Christians at Corinth, urges: 'Examine yourselves to see whether you are living in the faith. Test yourselves. Do you not realize that Jesus Christ is in you?—unless, indeed, you fail to pass the test!' (2 Corinthians 13:5).

There are at least two ways of defining a Christian. One is to see Jesus as your example, the model of all that is good and pure to which you aspire. The other is to experience the Spirit of Jesus living within you. Both are biblical definitions. The latter is captured by John in a vision in the Book of Revelation when he hears the Spirit of Jesus say: 'I reprove and discipline those whom I love. Be earnest, therefore, and repent. Listen! I am standing at the door, knocking; if you hear my voice and open the door, I will come in to you and eat with you, and you with me' (Revelation 3:19, 20). These words were spoken to church people in a city called Laodicea. They challenged them to adopt a spirituality that experienced the indwelling of God's Spirit. Many of us who go to church often lack this dynamic experience. The simple solution is to take Jesus at his word and, like the Jewish worshippers who opened wide the gates of the temple, open the door of your heart and let the King of Glory come in. There and then you will 'receive the blessing from the Lord'. For, what is blessing other than communion with the King of Glory?

A WORD *from* JESUS

Jesus said,

> 'Those who love me will keep my word, and my Father will love them, and we will come to them and make our home with them' (John 14:23).

A MEDITATION

Imagine a door to our inner being, your soul, your heart.
This is the place of your dreams,
your ambitions,
your feelings,
your will.
Imagine Jesus standing beyond the door, as the King of Glory. Imagine his light shining all around you. Imagine the door of your heart closed to him, shutting out the light.
Imagine the darkness that shrouds your dreams,
your ambitions,
your feelings,
your will.
Weep for the gates that bar the King of Glory.
Say:
'Lift up your heads, O gates!
and be lifted up, O ancient doors!
that the King of Glory may come in.'
Open the gates. Open wide the door of your heart.
The king of glory shall come in.
The king of glory has come in.
Hallelujah!

The BLESSING
of FORGIVENESS

PSALM 32:1–5

Blessed is he
whose transgressions are forgiven,
whose sins are covered.
Blessed is the man
whose sin the Lord does not count against him
and in whose spirit is no deceit.

When I kept silent,
my bones wasted away
through my groaning all day long.
For day and night
your hand was heavy upon me;
my strength was sapped
as in the heat of summer.
Then I acknowledged my sin to you
and did not cover up my iniquity.
I said, 'I will confess
my transgressions to the Lord'—
and you forgave
the guilt of my sin.

The PROMISE *of* BLESSING

Blessed is he
whose transgressions are forgiven,
whose sins are covered.

A REFLECTION

When I was a vicar I used to lead groups for those exploring the Christian faith. In one such group we were talking about God's offer of forgiveness when someone objected, 'Why do you keep emphasizing forgiveness? I don't need forgiveness.' I was startled as this person interrupted my flow of Christian doctrine, and was reminded yet again of the chasm that exists between Christians and those who do not share their view of the world. I gathered myself and lobbed a measured question by return.

'Have you never hurt another human being?'

'Oh, yes, of course,' she replied, more subdued.

'Then surely you need the forgiveness of those you've hurt. And you need the forgiveness of the one who made you.'

Our experience of the need for forgiveness is known by another word, guilt. Unfortunately, this idea has fallen on hard times. Some dismiss guilt as a neurosis. Some criticize Christianity for placing an unhealthy emphasis on guilt in order to keep people in the church. But guilt is the normal experience of men and women who are morally responsible for themselves. Some may wallow in guilt; some may experience guilt out of all proportion to their wrongdoing. These conditions may well be described as neurotic and require therapy. But a morally healthy human being ought to experience guilt when he does something wrong. Let's take an extreme example. If a rapist when convicted acknowledges no sense of guilt at his appalling crime then he is even less of a human being than his actions reveal. It is our human experience of guilt that paradoxically reveals our dignity as morally responsible persons. Although our culture is very coy about guilt and some counsellors dismiss it as unhealthy, the Bible clearly sees it as essential to our humanity.

All of us experience the need for forgiveness. There is not one soul on the face of the earth who has not needlessly hurt another person. We all need forgiveness. We all know what guilt is. 'Transgressions' means kicking over the traces. 'Trespassers will be prosecuted.' There is a line and nobody is allowed to go beyond it. If anyone crosses the line, he is a trespasser, a transgressor. God has drawn the line for us in the Ten Commandments and the Sermon on the Mount. Anyone who violates these laws is a trespasser and transgressor and needs God's forgiveness.

The good news which is trailed here and the broadcast by Jesus is that God is *willing* to forgive us. I used to think that God was a reluctant forgiver but when I became a father I discovered otherwise. Whenever my children kick over the traces and deliberately do something wrong I create a situation so that they can say sorry, so that I can forgive them, and we can be one again. God does not begrudge us his forgiveness. On the contrary, the extravagant generosity of his love impelled him to give us Jesus, our saviour and forgiver.

The picture given to us in this psalm is that the unforgiven soul is a restless, peaceless and dis-eased creature. The symptoms of his spiritual malaise are even physical. But God's forgiveness is there for the asking. Many of us seek peace for our souls in the strangest of places. It is only in journeying to 'the green hill' of Calvary, where we find our Lord crucified, that we find the forgiveness of our sins, the remission of our guilt and peace eternal for our souls. Will you come? There is blessing to be found.

A WORD *from* JESUS

After a sinful woman had anointed and bathed his feet at the house of Simon the Pharisee,

> Then he said to her, 'Your sins are forgiven... go in peace'
> (Luke 7:48, 50).

A PRAYER

Lord,
I have kept silent too long.
I have presumed upon your kindness.
I have left undone those things I should have done
and have done those things I should not have done.
I have kicked over the traces
through my own deliberate fault.
I have spoken words of destruction.
I have painted pictures with my mind
that would shame my closest friend.
I have done that which is evil in your sight.
Peace and blessing have been strangers to me.

Instead of seeking your face I have sought excuses.
Instead of confessing my transgression
I have sought to justify myself.
Instead of coveting your forgiveness
I have comforted myself with vanities:
'It's natural', 'I'm human', 'Everybody is like it'.
Lord, I confess my transgression.

Lord Jesus, have mercy on me.

My child,
I forgive you.
The guilt is gone.
Go in peace.
The blessing is yours.
Rejoice.

LEARNING of GOD

UNDERSTANDING HOLINESS

PSALM 32:8–11

I will instruct you and teach you in the way you should go;
I will counsel you and watch over you.
Do not be like the horse or the mule,
which have no understanding
but must be controlled by bit and bridle
or they will not come to you.
Many are the woes of the wicked,
but the Lord's unfailing love
surrounds the man who trusts in him.

Rejoice in the Lord and be glad, you righteous;
sing, all you who are upright in heart!

The PROMISE *of* BLESSING

Blessed is the man
whose sin the Lord does not count against him
and in whose spirit is no deceit.

A REFLECTION

There is an assumption here that God has the right to count our sins against us, to hold us accountable, to weigh us in the balances and find us wanting.

In the New Testament there are only four nouns used to describe God. God is light; God is Spirit; God is love (occurs only twice in the Bible) and God is a consuming fire. This last description holds before our eyes a vision of God's caustic purity. God burns with inextinguishable passion at every unjust desecration of his creation. The images of injustice—the hungry child, the mutilated murder victim, the masses of refugees—evoke outrage from us who are flawed. These images provoke God not to whisper some gentle rebuke but to shout a raucous and emphatic 'NO'. This is the holiness of God. He is at odds with both social injustice and personal immorality. He is separate from them. He is holy.

The holiness of God is not in vogue. Preachers and writers present a much more accommodating God. The God of today is visually handicapped, turning a blind eye to the indiscretions of his creatures.

We shall see in our final section of readings the lavish extent of God's grace; how he freely forgives. But forgiveness presupposes that someone has done something wrong and offensive to God's character. The doctrine of forgiveness presupposes a doctrine of holiness. Regrettably we feed ourselves with a diet of divine acceptance. God does accept us but it is *through* the forgiveness he offers. Is this merely playing with theological words? I think not. The idea that God simply accepts one and all is initially attractive. Certainly it is a healthy corrective to the pitiless God damning everyone in sight. But if the doctrine of divine acceptance is advanced *without* an emphasis on God's holiness and forgiveness it can lead to a situation where there is no serious moral change in the believer. If God accepts us warts and all, why go through the pain of cauterizing the warts? If God accepts us willy-nilly, why bother with the sweat of repentance, of changing one's attitude and way of life?

The reluctance to speak authoritatively about the holiness of God is one of the reasons why the church risks being so ineffectual: our churches do not bear the hallmarks of either social or personal holiness.

In order to change, we need to be conscious of how much we wrong God. The motivation to be different does not come from having to secure his favour but finds its source in knowing how holy God is and what it costs him to forgive us and so accept us. The doctrine of acceptance on its own leads to a God made in our image and likeness. The biblical doctrines of holiness, forgiveness and acceptance, however, lead to a willingness to be instructed in the way of holiness.

The sinner finds blessing not only in the forgiveness of the God who does not count his sin against him but also in the experience of God instructing, teaching and correcting him in holiness.

A WORD *from* JESUS

Jesus said to his disciples,

> 'Be perfect, therefore, as your heavenly Father is perfect'
> (Matthew 5:48).

A PRAYER

Wilt thou forgive that sinne where I begunne,
Which was my sin, though it were done before?
Wilt thou forgive those sinnes, through which I runne,
And do run still: though still I do deplore?
When thou hast done, thou hast not done,
For, I have more.

Wilt thou forgive that sinne by which I have wonne
Others to sinne? and, made my sinne their doore?
Wilt thou forgive that sinne which I did shunne
A yeare, or two: but wallowed in, a score?
When thou hast done, thou hast not done,
For I have more.

I have a sinne of feare, that when I have spunne
My last thred, I shall perish on the shore;
Sweare by thy selfe, that at my death thy sonne
Shall shine as he shines now, and heretofore;
And, having done that, Thou hast done,
I feare no more.

John Donne, 1572–1631

NATIONAL BLESSING

PSALM 33:1–12

Rejoice in the Lord, O you righteous!
Praise befits the upright.
Praise the Lord with the lyre,
make melody to him with the harp of ten strings!
Sing to him a new song,
play skilfully on the strings, with loud shouts.

For the word of the Lord is upright;
and all his work is done in faithfulness.
He loves righteousness and justice;
the earth is full of the steadfast love of the Lord.

By the word of the Lord the heavens were made,
and all their host by the breath of his mouth.
He gathered the waters of the sea as in a bottle;
he put the deeps in storehouses.

Let all the earth fear the Lord,
let all the inhabitants of the world stand in awe of him!
For he spoke, and it came to be;
he commanded, and it stood forth.

The Lord brings the counsel of the nations to naught;
he frustrates the plans of the peoples.
The counsel of the Lord stands for ever,
the thoughts of his heart to all generations.
Blessed is the nation whose God is the Lord,
the people whom he has chosen as his heritage!

The PROMISE *of* BLESSING

Blessed is the nation whose God is the Lord,
the people whom he has chosen as his heritage!

A REFLECTION

Blessing is not to be a purely private experience: an individual's experience of God is personal not least in the experience of forgiveness: but this verse extends the promise of blessing beyond the individual and this psalm reveals that God deals with national communities as well as with individual persons.

The nation in mind here is Israel. Theirs was a history of endurance and deliverance—oppressed one moment, rescued the next. Never always oppressed, never always free. In all of these experiences, they learned to see the hand of the Lord and sing his praise:

> *Happy are you, O Israel! Who is like you,*
> *a people saved by the Lord,*
> *the shield of your help,*
> *and the sword of your triumph! (Deuteronomy 33:29)*

But can the experiences of Israel apply to other nations? Does the promise of national blessing extend beyond the Israel of the Old Testament to the nations of our modern world?

In the second half of the twentieth century two movements developed that concerned themselves with how God deals with nations, namely liberation theology and the Moral Majority. Liberation theology argued that the universal struggle for justice had a biblical basis and a divine mandate. The Moral Majority in the United States pressed politically for a society established on biblical principles. Put like that, one might wonder if there were any difference at all between the two. Both appealed to the Bible; both were convinced that there was a connection between the spiritual and the temporal; both sensed a divine call to influence the world with their biblical manifesto. But politically these two movements were poles apart.

As Christians we must be cautious about the danger of imposing a political agenda on the Bible. We must be wary of using the Bible to support our political prejudices and we must resist baptizing any political movement as God's army. Societies require different policies as they develop. If a society pursues a programme of *laissez-faire* so that the poor suffer then the Church must speak authoritatively from the Bible of the moral obligation God lays on the strong to care for the poor. If a society pursues a programme of collectivism so that there is no freedom, neither political nor economic nor religious, for the individual, then the Church must speak out against that oppression.

The Church's response in the world will, therefore, vary from culture to culture and focus upon different needs and circumstances. To this extent, the Church's role is largely practical but it also has a wider responsibility to bring before the nation the universal laws of God about freedom and truth, justice and mercy that are binding on all peoples because he is their creator. The Church consequently will never be popular with politicians. A prophet has never been a politician's best friend.

The New Testament recognizes that God places the Church, 'a holy nation, God's own people', in national communities and insists that Christians pray for those in civil and national leadership (1 Peter 2). The outcome of this prophetic witness and prayer is that God might bless the nation with that which is good:

> *He has told you, O mortal, what is good;*
> *and what does the Lord require of you*
> *but to do justice, and to love kindness,*
> *and to walk humbly with your God? (Micah 6:8)*

God entered a contract with Israel and made that nation a people for his own possession. *Through Jesus God extends the contract of possession to all nations.*

The mission of God is one of possession, making disciples of all nations just as he discipled the nation of Israel. Our nation no longer acknowledges (did it ever truly?) the Lord as its God. The church's mission through personal evangelism and social renewal is to make the nation a people for God's own possession, or 'heritage'. A nation possessed by God. A nation blessed.

A WORD *from* JESUS

Jesus assured his disciples of his everlasting presence and left them with this message after the resurrection:

> *All authority in heaven and on earth has been given to me. Go therefore and make disciples of all nations, baptizing them... and teaching them to obey everything that I have commanded you... (Matthew 28:19, 20)*

A MEDITATION

In your imagination soar like a bird over the place where you live. As you see familiar sights, homes of peoples you know, schools, institutions, police stations, local government buildings, television studios, banks, say each time, 'Blessed is the nation whose God is the Lord.' Then re-read the psalm.

Next time you watch or hear a news bulletin respond to each item in your heart with the words, 'Blessed is the nation whose God is the Lord.'

TASTING *the* LORD

PSALM 34:1—10

I will bless the Lord continually:
his praise shall be always in my mouth.
Let my soul boast of the Lord:
the humble shall hear it and rejoice.
O praise the Lord with me:
let us exalt his name together

For I sought the Lord's help and he answered:
and he freed me from all my fears.
Look towards him and be bright with joy:
your faces shall not be ashamed.
Here is a wretch who cried and the Lord heard him:
and saved him from all his troubles.
The angel of the Lord encamps round those who fear him:
and delivers them in their need.
O taste and see that the Lord is good:
happy the man who hides in him!
Fear the Lord all you his holy ones:
for those who fear him never lack.
Lions may suffer want and go hungry:
but those who seek the Lord lack nothing good.

The PROMISE of BLESSING

O taste and see that the Lord is good:
happy the man who hides in him.

A REFLECTION

Taste and see

Like most people I'm hesitant about eating food I've never had before. The first mouthful is always very tentative as we 'taste and see'. I once heard somebody on the radio recommend that strawberries should be eaten without sugar and cream but with pepper. I was intrigued. The following summer I tried it. I ground some black pepper on to a plate and to the consternation of the other guests gently trailed the strawberry in the condiment. I lifted the berry to my lips, sniffed, but not too deeply, and bit a morsel of the pointed end. I kept it in the front of my mouth, savouring the flavour and, when confident that all was well, swallowed. Not bad: indeed, quite extraordinary. The pepper uniquely drew out the flavour of the strawberry. The other guests joined in. Should you be intrigued by this recipe and decide to try one for yourself, then I should imagine that you would, like me, approach the first taste with caution.

All tasting is tentative. When in the psalm we read about tasting and seeing that the Lord is good there is a recognition here by God that our first steps of faith are themselves tentative. We respond to the call to put our trust in God with caution. Even as Christians we find ourselves in new situations which call us to trust God again in a new way. We are not quite sure at first whether this will be a good experience for us and we hesitate nervously. But buoyed up by the encouragement of other Christians, or exhausted by the pressures of life, we take the first tentative step. To our surprise it is not bad. Like a newborn baby who finds intuitively his mother's breast and sucks her milk until satisfied, so, too, we, who have tentatively tasted the goodness of the Lord, go on thirsting and drinking more deeply (1 Peter 2:2, 3).

Happy the man who hides in him

This psalm shows that the life of a Christian is a bed of roses with thorns: there are moments of beauty but there are times of troubles. Just as Israel's story was one of endurance and deliverance so the story of every Christian is a similar blend. Throughout our life we will experience a cycle of endurance and deliverance—Good Friday followed by Easter Sunday. Life is not one long Good

Friday. Nor is it a perpetual Easter Sunday.

When the troubles come we are to hide. In all the latter day titles given to Jesus such as 'the Radical Jesus', 'Christ the Controversialist', 'the Compassionate Jesus', 'Jesus, Man of Prayer', there is one that I have never seen: 'The Hiding Jesus'. Yet on several occasions Jesus hides to avoid confrontation and on many occasions he deliberately retreats. When bereaved by the death of his cousin, John, the grieving Jesus goes away to be on his own. When people try to force his hand and make him king, Jesus doesn't stay to confront the issue but hides in the hills. Jesus withdraws. Here is an example for us to follow. It is not dishonourable to hide. There is a time to face the enemy and a time to retreat from the heat of battle. This psalm promises blessing to those who make the Lord their hiding-place.

In this hiding-place we can take stock of our situation and begin to look at our problems as God sees them. The problems do not change, yet often our relationship to them changes. Instead of feeling submerged and panic-stricken, we can become more detached and view the difficulties more objectively. By taking ourselves out of the situation and by placing ourselves consciously in the presence of God we can begin to open ourselves up to the inexhaustible influence of the Holy Spirit who gives power and strength to the faint and weary.

A WORD *from* JESUS

Jesus said,

> *'Come away to a deserted place all by yourselves and rest a while'* (Mark 6:31).

A MEDITATION

The Revd Augustus Toplady was riding across the hills of Somerset when a storm broke. He took shelter from the fierce elements in the cleft of a great rock and hid. As he sheltered in the safety of the rock from the wind and the rain he began to meditate on another hiding place, the Rock of Ages.

> *Rock of Ages, cleft for me*
> *Let me hide myself in thee;*

Let the water and the blood
From thy riven side which flowed,
Be of sin the double cure
Cleanse me from its guilt and power.

Nothing in my hand I bring,
Simply to thy cross I cling;
Naked, come to thee for dress,
Helpless, look to thee for grace;
Foul, I to the fountain fly,
Wash me, Saviour, or I die.

Recall the last time you were caught in a storm. How did you shelter from it? Dwell on this memory and in it see a picture of the Lord sheltering you from all the assaults of your enemies. Repeat slowly this promise: 'Blessed is the one who hides in you.'

BIBLICAL COMMUNITY

PSALM 37:1–7, 20–28

Do not worry about the wicked,
do not envy those who do wrong.
Quick as the grass they wither,
fading like the green in the field.

Trust in Yahweh and do what is good,
make your home in the land and live in peace;
make Yahweh your only joy
and he will give you what your heart desires.

Commit your fate to Yahweh,
trust in him and he will act:
making your virtue clear as the light,
your integrity as bright as noon.

Be quiet before Yahweh, and wait patiently for him,
not worrying about men who make their fortunes,
about men who scheme
to bring the poor and needy down...

As for the wicked—they will perish,
these enemies of Yahweh;
they will vanish like the beauty of the meadows,
they will vanish in smoke.

The wicked man borrows without meaning to repay,
but a virtuous man is generous and open-handed;
those he blesses will have the land for their own,
those he curses will be expelled.

Yahweh guides a man's steps,
they are sure, and he takes pleasure in his progress;

he may fall, but never fatally,
since Yahweh supports him by the hand.

Now I am old, but ever since my youth
I never saw a virtuous man deserted,
or his descendants forced to beg their bread;
he is always compassionate, always lending:
his children will be blessed.

Never yield to evil, practise good
and you will have an everlasting home,
for Yahweh loves what is right,
and never deserts the devout.

The PROMISE *of* BLESSING

Now I am old, but ever since my youth
I never saw a virtuous man deserted,
or his descendants forced to beg their bread;
he is always compassionate, always lending:
his children will be blessed.

A REFLECTION

I remember visiting an old people's home just before Christmas. I asked a chair-bound lady whom I knew well when her children would be collecting her for Christmas Day. 'Oh,' she explained, trying to inject control into her emotional reply, 'well, you know they're very busy. They've got the children now. I'd just be in the way. Anyway it's too long a journey. They'll come sometime.' As the lady struggled to excuse her son I began to see how easy it is in our society to forget our responsibilities to our elderly relatives. The mother was in a comfortable home. They were a distance away. These factors conspired all too easily with the individualism of our culture that permits people to see themselves primarily as single individuals rather than as family members. This culture of ours is a different world from that of the Bible.

In both the Old and New Testaments people are seen as members of a family community. The blessing that comes to the head of the family comes to all the household including children. Even in the New Testament the blessing of salvation comes to the whole household. Jesus assures Zacchaeus when he repents of his fraud and promises to make reparation that salvation has come not just to him but to the whole house (Luke 19:9). And in Acts, when Paul urges the jailer to believe in the Lord Jesus, he promises that not only he but his whole house will be saved on his confession of faith (Acts 16:31). In his book, *Christianity Rediscovered* (SCM 1978), Vincent Donovan tells of his evangelistic work with the Masai. When the moment for baptism comes Donovan selects those he deems suitable. He embarks upon the selection process and is promptly informed by the Chief that he will baptize either all of them or none of them. This African people took Donovan back to a biblical pattern of community which he and we are blind to through our ungodly individualism.

This psalm rehearses a biblical principle that God places us in a family. By this we do not mean that he locates us all in a unit of mother, father and 2.6 children. Rather, we are born into a community, we are raised in a community and it is through this community of persons that we learn how to love and be loved and so discover our worth. Individuals deprived of such a community of loving when growing up find it difficult to hold themselves in any esteem, to love and allow themselves to be loved. Whether the family community is mother, father and 2.6 children or a single-parent household, it is love that shapes the emotional development and maturity of its members.

This psalm speaks of one who delights in God. Resisting the distractions of those who seem successfully to ignore God, the psalmist makes the Lord his only joy. As he does so he experiences the open-handed generosity of God. He knows God's love and compassion for himself. So he in turn, moulded and shaped by the grace of God, becomes a compassionate and generous person. Needless to say, it is his own children who benefit from his virtue. It is at his knee and in his arms that they first feel love and discover that they are lovable. It is through their parents that they learn how much they are worth. And how much they are worth to God. It is in this way that God's blessing begins to flow to our children.

You may object that there are many religious people who have the most awkward and irreligious children. I have met them. Two points are worth adding. Firstly, the children of Christians will, like all young people who move from adolescence to adulthood, need to stretch their wings and make their first traumatic flights from the nest. Secondly, religious people often have the form but not the content of a personal relationship with God and our children are the first to see it. Such a warning should drive us all back to this psalm to 'make Yahweh your only joy and he will give you the desires of your heart'.

Then we shall become a blessing to our children, to our family, to our friends and even to our enemies.

A WORD *from* JESUS

At the Last Supper, Jesus said,

> 'As the Father has loved me, so I have loved you; abide in my love...
> This is my commandment, that you love one another as I have loved
> you' (John 15:9, 12).

A SPIRITUAL EXERCISE

When Jesus says 'abide in my love', he is inviting us to experience heaven.

No man can possibly be happy in a place where he is not in his element, and where all around him is not congenial to his tastes, habits, and character. When an eagle is happy in an iron cage, when a sheep is happy in the water, when an owl is happy in the blaze of noonday sun, when a fish is happy on the dry land—then, and not till then, will I admit that the unsanctified man could be happy in heaven. (J.C. Ryle, Holiness, 1879)

The invitation to abide in the heavenly love of Christ is a challenge to our 'tastes, habits, and character'. Take time to examine yourself.

LEARNING PATIENCE

PSALM 40:1–5

I waited patiently for the Lord;
he inclined to me and heard my cry.
He drew me up from the desolate pit,
out of the miry bog,
and set me feet upon a rock,
making my steps secure.
He put a new song in my mouth,
a song of praise to our God.
Many will see and fear,
and put their trust in the Lord.

Blessed is the man who makes
the Lord his trust,
who does not turn to the proud,
to those who go astray after false gods!
Thou hast multiplied, O Lord my God,
thy wondrous deeds and thy thoughts toward us;
none can compare with thee!
Were I to proclaim and tell of them,
they would be more than can be numbered.

The PROMISE *of* BLESSING

Blessed is the man who makes
the Lord his trust,
who does not turn to the proud,
to those who go astray after false gods!

A REFLECTION

Waiting does not come easily to any of us. The difficulty is accentuated through living in that part of the world where so much of what is offered is instantly available—from credit to coffee, we can have it in an instant. E-mail and the Internet have eliminated distance. We have immediate access to so much. We are getting more and more unaccustomed to waiting for anything and the virtue of patience is in short supply. I find myself always in the wrong queue. When checking out of a supermarket I try to assess carefully the quickest queue by seeing not only how many people are lining up but also how much is in their trolleys. Invariably, having joined the queue, someone in front has a problem with their cheque or the assistant can't find the price of an item and I stand there fuming as other queues sail through. No patience. Whether it is choosing a queue in the bank or a line of traffic I do not have the patience to wait. Why can't we just relax and accept our situations?

I was once queuing for a telephone in a motorway service station and getting increasingly impatient with the thoughtlessness of the talkative person using the telephone, ignoring the length of the queue outside. Eventually I rang home and continued my journey ten minutes later than expected. Further along the motorway I passed the most appalling accident. Police and ambulances were already on the scene of an accident that had happened only minutes earlier. It crossed my mind where I might have been now had there been no queue for the telephone.

Much of our impatience stems from a self-centred view of the world. We observe our situation and in our pride think that we know best. When the situation is not resolved immediately we cast around for alternatives which we reckon will serve our best interests. But where is the evidence that we are omniscient of every detail and know what is best? I would have thought that most of us have sufficient life-experience to know that the evidence points in the opposite direction.

Whether it is queuing in a line of traffic or waiting for the next development in a career, whether holding on in the process of moving house or waiting for someone to agree with your plans, whether waiting for the children as they gaze in wonder at some new sight or waiting for the proverbial pot to boil, *patience is a virtue*. God is not calling us to be fatalistic; faith is not fate running its course, but consciously committing situations to God and learning to see them with God at the centre instead of yourself.

Faith is a wilful offloading of the outcome into God's hands and learning to accept that he knows best. Faith is resolutely refusing to change horses mid-stream once you have committed all to God. In the period of waiting, many doubts will arise. The false god of 'Instant Now' will question the wisdom of waiting with a very plausible appeal to your ego. He will whisper phrases like ,'You've *waited* long enough'; 'How much longer are you going to *wait*?' He will make you feel that waiting is a vice, something that will do you injury, something that will rob you of the best. But don't go after this false god. Instead, follow the psalmist's example: wait and wait and keep on waiting. That is what the first verse means. Don't give up. Make the Lord your trust.

A WORD *from* JESUS

'No one who puts a hand to the plough and looks back is fit for the kingdom of God' (Luke 9:62).

A PAUSE *for* THOUGHT

Recall the last time you were successfully impatient and saved yourself some time. What did you do with the time you saved?

WORKING *for the* POOR

PSALM 41:1–13

Blessed is he that considers the poor and the helpless:
the Lord will deliver him in the day of trouble.
The Lord will guard him and preserve his life
he shall be counted happy in the land:
you will not give him over to the will of his enemies.
And if he lies sick on his bed the Lord will sustain him:
if illness lays him low you will overthrow it.

I said 'O Lord be merciful toward me:
heal me for I have sinned against you.'
My enemies speak evil of me saying:
'When will he die and his name perish for ever?'
And if one should come to see me he mouths empty words:
while his heart gathers mischief
and when he goes out he vents it.
All those that hate me whisper together against me:
they devise plots against me.

They say 'A deadly thing has got hold of him:
he will not get up again from where he lies.'
Even my bosom friend in whom I trusted:
who shared my bread has lifted his heel against me.
But you O Lord be gracious and raise me up:
and I will repay them what they have deserved.

By this will I know that you favour me:
that my enemies shall not triumph over me.
Because of my innocence you hold me fast:
you have set me before your face for ever.

Blessed be the Lord the God of Israel:
from everlasting to everlasting. Amen. Amen.

The PROMISE *of* BLESSING

Blessed is he that considers the poor and the helpless:
the Lord will deliver him in the day of trouble.

A REFLECTION

Over forty years ago a person emigrated to Britain from the Caribbean. His mother told him exactly what to do when he got here. 'First, find a church—so you can thank God. Second, find a post office—so you can write home. Then, find a friend.' He found the post office quite easily, but sadly this man and many others found few friends in either this country or its many churches. Consequently, these people formed their own church and the man became one of their bishops.

At that moment in the history of our church, for all the high and lofty sentiment of our theology and our preaching, very few of us were considering the poor and the helpless: the separation of black brothers and sisters has deprived this nation's church of one of God's blessings.

The Old Testament is full of the love of God. It is here that we learn to love our neighbour as ourself (Leviticus 19:18), to hate injustice as God hates all oppression (Leviticus 19:13), to protect ethnic groups (Leviticus 19:10) and to look after the weak and helpless (Psalm 41:1). These sounds of compassion are echoed throughout the Old Testament by the prophets of the God who is full of compassion. We cannot drive a wedge between the Old and New Testaments: they both reveal the love of God and both teach us our duty concerning the poor.

Helping the poor sometimes takes us out on a limb—we can feel lonely and unsupported. We might start off some enterprise with a group of people but gradually the others become uninterested and we are left on our own. The experience can make us wary of ever getting involved again. This psalm encourages me for it gives an example of someone who starts to take seriously the plight of the distressed and to do something about it, only to find himself laid up and beset with problems. I have sometimes felt very let down by God when, having gone out of my way to help someone, things have started going wrong for me. I would have thought that by doing something so clearly approved by him, God would have ensured a smoother passage. But the way of Christ is different. Helping the poor does not guarantee you either popularity or good fortune in this life. Jesus himself made this discovery. He spent himself. And when Judas emerged to inflict thorns on his head and wounds on his body, Jesus quoted from this psalm: '"The one who ate my bread has lifted his heel against me"' (John 13:18). We sometimes pray to walk in the footsteps of Jesus. But like the mother of James and John who wanted greatness and glory for her sons, Jesus cautions us, 'You do not know what you are asking.' Christianity without tears is not what is on offer to those who follow Jesus. It is only beyond the grave that God will wipe away all the tears.

To follow him, to work for the poor and helpless, will not immunize us from hardship. And if you are struggling at this moment with some burden, read carefully. Maybe you're exhausted in caring for a dependent relative, or supporting someone stricken by grief; maybe you live with someone in the depths of depression, or are running a support group for single-parent families; maybe you're strengthening someone bereaved through divorce, or fighting the local council to right a wrong. Perhaps you feel you've had enough, for your own problems have increased. Stay with it.

But, you protest, what about the blessing that is on offer here? It takes the insights of Jesus to appreciate fully what the psalmist promises. Those who have fed the hungry, made the stranger welcome, clothed the destitute and visited prisoners are to hear Jesus saying to their surprise: 'Truly I say to you, as you did it to one of the least of these my brethren, you did it to me.' And here is the blessing: to see Jesus in the face of the helpless. Blessing is certainly a future experience. Heaven is the consummate blessing. But blessing is also a present gift, for any meeting with Jesus is a blessing. All encounters with God are blessings. May we all look with eyes bathed in the lotion of scripture to see that whenever we consider the poor we behold the face of Jesus. What a deprivation we have endured for failing to see whom we have turned away by rejecting our brothers and sisters.

A WORD *from* JESUS

To the crowds gathered to hear his teaching, Jesus proclaimed,

'Blessed are the merciful, for they will receive mercy' (Matthew 5:7).

A MEDITATION

Think of someone whom you are helping. Allow to surface any resentment, anger, hostility and frustration. Freely express all this to God. Ask God to forgive you of any sin. Hold the image of the person in your mind and hear the words of Jesus repeating themselves: 'You did it to me.' Relax and spend time thanking God for this vision.

Now hear these words from Jesus: 'Come, O blessed of my Father, inherit the kingdom.'

INSPIRED *by* ROYALTY

PSALM 45:1—12

My heart is astir with fine phrases,
I make my song for a king:
my tongue is the pen of a ready writer.

You are the fairest of the sons of men,
grace flows from your lips:
therefore God has blessed you for ever and ever.
Gird your sword upon your thigh, O mighty warrior:
in glory and majesty tread down your foes and triumph!

Ride on in the cause of truth:
and for the sake of justice.
Your right hand shall teach a terrible instruction:
peoples shall fall beneath you,
your arrows shall be sharp in the hearts of the king's enemies.

Your throne is the throne of God, it endures for ever:
and the sceptre of your kingdom is a righteous sceptre.
You have loved righteousness and hated evil:
therefore God your God has anointed you
with the oil of gladness above your fellows.
All your garments are fragrant with myrrh, aloes and cassia:
music from ivory palaces makes you glad.
Kings' daughters are among your noble women:
the queen is at your right hand in gold of Ophir.

Hear O daughter, consider and incline your ear:
forget your own people and your father's house.
The king desires your beauty:
he is your lord, therefore bow down before him.
The richest among the people, O daughter of Tyre:
shall entreat your favour with gifts.

The PROMISE *of* BLESSING

You are the fairest of the sons of men
grace flows from your lips:
therefore God has blessed you for ever and ever.

A REFLECTION

This psalm was inspired by a royal wedding. The eyes of the people were on the groom and his bride. It was a splendid occasion of beautiful pageant and glorious ritual.

Although it ended in tragedy, I am sure that most of those who watched the marriage of Prince Charles and Lady Diana Spencer will never forget it. Over five hundred million people watched their wedding in St Paul's Cathedral. I remember sitting in a mountain chalet in Switzerland enjoying the spectacle on the television with a number of people from different countries. We were all absorbed by the colourful celebration and awesome solemnity. The cheering, jubilant crowds thronged the Mall. The sober and well-marshalled guests and officials filled the Cathedral. The cameras captured both, and the commentator's whispering voice unfolded for us the drama in which the bride was led to the church to stand by her prince. In the presence of God and before this congregation of five hundred million people Charles and Diana made their vows and exchanged solemn promises. Millions of people from all over the world and many cultural backgrounds were being bound together in this vision. Their imaginations exploring what it must be like for Her and Him, and wondering perhaps what they themselves would feel if they were the Prince and Princess.

There was universal sadness that the marriage which began like a fairy tale should have ended in such tragedy. Diana's death disturbed the world and drew the grief of millions. Some so sad they grieved more for her than for their own relatives. Through mourning her death it was as if people were being given permission to grieve over other losses. Her death made people feel vulnerable: if one so beautiful, famous, glamorous, fit and wealthy could not be protected from the tunnel of death, then who was safe? Suddenly her death made everyone feel their mortality. In the international grief there was, as in all personal grief, depression, anger and guilt. A gloom shrouded London like a funeral pall. Anger was directed at the Queen and focused on the absence of a half-mast flag over Buckingham Palace. The Queen, hitherto eclipsed by two imposing women, Lady Thatcher and the Princess of Wales, came again into her own as mother of the nation absorbing the anger of her grief-stricken people. And the guilt. The queues of mourners in London and around the world who signed books of condolence were driven by different emotions. But most had at some time gazed on a forbidden photograph snapped and snatched illicitly by highly-paid paparazzi. The ritual silent queuing was the only sacrifice open to them to atone for their complicity in her death, pursued by photographers.

In the persons and the events of the Royal Family we find our representatives. In many ways they are very different from ourselves, not least because of their wealth and privilege and the necessary security by which they live. But in those universal moments of life which embrace us all—birth, marriage and death—members of the Royal Family speak for us all when they celebrate, when they make solemn promises, and when they grieve. They, too, know the pain of childbirth, the nervous excitement of getting married, and the depression of grief. Wealth, privilege and security do not shield them from these human experiences and their intense emotions. In these moments of hatching, matching and despatching they are one with us all. We know what it is like for them and they know what it is like for us. So when a royal baby is born, a royal couple married, a royal person dies, it is the talk of the town. Suddenly an opportunity has been triggered for us to talk freely and fully of these experiences. It is as if some psychoanalyst-in-the-sky has held before his corporate patient some picture, some image, some word that releases deep emotion that has been longing for expression.

So in this psalm the king's marriage stirs the poet. The pen is poised: fine phrases flow. The noble theme is expressed with feeling. Down the centuries and ever since the wonders of the New Testament, the king in this psalm has reminded Christians of Jesus. Like any royal personage he is both different from us and one with us. He is the God who knows what it is like to be human. He does not observe pain at a safe distance. He has experienced the grief and the joy, the tears and the laughter, the agony and the ecstasy of being human. When we see Jesus crying we know that we need not be ashamed of our tears. When we see Jesus rejoicing we know that we need not feel guilty about enjoying ourselves. Here is our representative. He holds before us and draws from within us all that is good about being human.

It is Jesus who is the fairest of the sons of men. And grace flows from his lips. God has blessed him for ever and ever. The good news for us is that God has blessed us through him.

A WORD *from* JESUS

As he was now approaching the path down from the Mount of Olives, the whole multitude of the disciples began to praise God joyfully with a loud voice for all the deeds of power that they had seen, saying,

'Blessed is the king who comes in the name of the Lord! Peace in heaven, and glory in the highest heaven!'

Some of the Pharisees in the crowd said to him, 'Teacher, order your disciples to stop.' He answered, 'I tell you, if these were silent, the stones would shout out' (Luke 19:37–40).

HYMN *of* PRAISE

You are the King of Glory,
You are the Prince of Peace,
You are the Lord of heav'n and earth,
You're the Son of righteousness.
Angels bow down before you,
Worship and adore,
For you have the words of eternal life,
You are Jesus Christ the Lord.

Hosanna to the Son of David!
Hosanna to the King of kings!
Glory in the highest heaven
For Jesus the Messiah reigns!

TRUSTING
in GOD

True Wealth

Psalm 49:5–19

Why should I fear in times of trouble,
when the iniquity of my persecutors surrounds me,
men who trust in their wealth
and boast of the abundance of their riches?
Truly no man can ransom himself,
or give to God the price of his life,
for the ransom of life is costly,
and can never suffice,
that he should continue to live on for ever,
and never see the Pit.

Yea, he shall see that even the wise die,
the fool and the stupid alike must perish
and leave their wealth to others.
Their graves are their homes for ever,
their dwelling places to all generations,
though they named lands their own.
Man cannot abide in his pomp,
he is like the beasts that perish.

This is the fate of those who have foolish confidence,
the end of those who are pleased with their portion.
Like sheep they are appointed for Sheol;
Death shall be their shepherd;
straight to the grave they descend,
and their form shall waste away;
Sheol shall be their home.
But God will ransom my soul from the power of Sheol,
for he will receive me.

The WARNING *of* BLESSING

Be not afraid when one becomes rich,
when the glory of his house increases.
For when he dies he will carry nothing away;
his glory will not go down after him.
Though, while he lives, he counts himself happy,
and though a man gets praise when he does well for himself,
he will go to the generation of his fathers,
who will never more see the light (Psalm 49:16–19).

A REFLECTION

After the funeral of a rich person the distant relatives and friends were enquiring among themselves as to how much the old man was worth. When the vicar passed and overheard one of them ask, 'How much did he leave?' he added with wit and truth, 'Everything!' It is good for Christians to remind themselves that they import and export nothing from this world. God has given us a material world to enjoy and for that we should daily give him thanks. But all of us know the power of money and the addiction of possessions. This psalm reminds us that wealth is ultimately extremely powerless. Money may well purchase the luxury of a fine house and, in today's world, it may provide you with better medical care and so extend your life a little, but money is powerless in staving off death: the rich and the poor die together.

People who are wealthy, however, seem to be happy. Their grass looks greener and it appears that they have their blessing without God. This was so in the time of David, of Jesus and in our own day. 'Godless' people who enjoy success have always unsettled men and women who have sought with tears to put God first. Although it is doubtful that the psalmist understood the full import of his words, the last verse points to a communion with God and a blessing beyond this life: 'But God will ransom my soul from the power of Sheol, for he will receive me.' For those of us disturbed by the apparent success of men and women who have no regard for God and no respect for his justice, the resurrection of Jesus shouts that there is more to life than those three score years and ten. It is in the light of eternity that the final judgments are to be made.

Traditionally, Lent used to be a time of renunciation, a time to give up some material luxury. This has gone out of fashion not least under theological influence that we should not live under the dualistic misapprehension that the material is bad and the spiritual good. This false division between spirit and matter has led the Church into all kinds of difficulties, especially in the fields of the arts, sexuality and politics. With a few notable exceptions Christians have been shy of entering into politics. And in so far as sex is concerned Christians are often heard being only negative. Nevertheless, there is a place for the following message: God's material creation is good but the enjoyment of it should never be pursued without the acknowledgment of God as the Provider. That is why it is appropriate at times like Lent to abstain from the material benefits and so remind ourselves of their origin. A measure of self-imposed abstinence can help us to shift our attention from the provisions to the provider.

A WORD *from* JESUS

Apart from the Kingdom of God Jesus spoke most about money and wealth.

> 'What will it profit them if they gain the whole world but forfeit their life?' (Matthew 16:26)

> 'Your heavenly Father knows that you need all these things. But strive first for the kingdom of God and his righteousness, and all these things will be given to you as well' (Matthew 6:33).

A MEDITATION

Let your mind focus on some beautiful aspect of God's creation. Imagine yourself painting or photographing the scene. Give thanks for this.

Then hear Jesus saying to you repeatedly, 'Are you not of more value?'

He Chooses Us

Psalm 65:1—6

Praise awaits you, O God, in Zion;
to you our vows will be fulfilled.
O you who hear prayer,
to you all men will come.
When we were overwhelmed by sins,
you made atonement for our transgressions.
Blessed are those you choose
and bring near to live in your courts!
We are filled with the good things of your house,
of your holy temple.

You answer us with awesome deeds of righteousness,
O God our Saviour,
the hope of all the ends of the earth
and of the farthest seas,
who formed the mountains by your power...

The Promise of Blessing

Blessed are those you choose
and bring near to live in your courts!

A Reflection

In choosing to live for God we discover that it is he who has chosen us. We tend to think that we are the ones who do all the deciding. But the more we live in the light of God's truth the more aware we become that it is he who stands at the centre of the universe and not us. It is he who does the beckoning and he who is the source of the magnetic field drawing all men and women to himself.

Just as a small child enters a playroom and, following his

imagination, explores the toys unaware that someone has laid it all out for his enjoyment, so we enter this world. Just as the small child opens the box of plasticene and with the shapes and cutters cannot resist creating his own world, so we make our own way in life. Like the child, we are unaware of the influences of another presence. But just as the child grows to recognize the evidence of the activity of another in his playroom so we begin to see the fingerprints of the Maker and to realize that we are caught up in a plot much thicker than we first thought. God is at work. Often we cannot see it at the time, but with hindsight we discern the hand of God.

The job of the Old Testament prophets was to interpret to the children of Israel their history and to help them to recognize the activity of God on their behalf. So God spoke through Moses: 'You have seen what I did to the Egyptians, and how I bore you on eagles' wings and brought you to myself. Now therefore, if you obey my voice and keep my covenant, you shall be my treasured possession... a priestly kingdom and a holy nation' (Exodus 19:4–6). God chose the children of Israel and blessed them.

God's choosing of the Israelites did not exonerate them from the responsibility of having daily to choose God for themselves, or immunize them from the trauma of living in a world terrorized by evil. The blessing of God's choosing was that the people of God were able to commune with him. The chief expression of their communion with God was to visit the temple. This building was a means of grace which 'filled them with good things'. Here they worshipped God freely; God heard their prayers and forgave their sins. The temple, filled with the sound of praise and the smell of atoning sacrifices, spoke to them of God their saviour. God, revealed to them in the temple, would one day more fully reveal himself in our Lord and saviour, Jesus Christ.

Just as the Israelites were able to look back over their lives to see with the eyes of faith how God was at work rescuing them, so we who are Christians ought to reflect on our own experience of God. What signs of his grace have you observed in your own life? When have you been aware that there was something going on beyond your own control? How did you respond when you sensed that God was choosing you to be his?

Worshipping in the house of God with the people of God is a

glorious experience but we do not have to wait for that moment to enjoy our communion with God. Here and now we can praise him, pray to him, and be assured of his forgiveness. Here and now we can know the blessing of having been chosen and brought into fellowship with our God and saviour.

A WORD *from* JESUS

Jesus said,

> 'You did not choose me but I chose you. And I appointed you to go and bear fruit, fruit that will last' (John 15:16).

A MEDITATION

You did not choose me, but I chose you

You chose me, O God.
You chose this sinner to praise you with songs of worship,
to promise solemn vows of obedience.

You chose me, O God.
You chose this sinner to hear his prayers
to atone for his transgressions.

You chose me, O God.
You chose this sinner to live in your presence
and to fill him with good things.

You chose me, O God.
And I thought that I had chosen you!
But you chose me,
You rescued me.
You delivered me out of the dominion of darkness
and into the glorious light of your presence.

Here I am.
Chosen.
Chosen and full of praise.
Chosen and promising obedience.
Chosen and heard.

Chosen and forgiven.
Chosen and in your presence.
Chosen and satisfied.
Chosen and blessed. Amen.

SHINE UPON US

PSALM 67:1–7

May God be gracious to us and bless us
and make his face to shine upon us,
that thy way may be known upon earth,
thy saving power among all nations.
Let the people praise thee, O God;
let all the peoples praise thee!

Let the nations be glad and sing for joy,
for thou dost judge the peoples with equity
and guide the nations upon the earth.
Let the peoples praise thee, O God;
let all the peoples praise thee!

The earth has yielded its increase;
God, our God, has blessed us.
God has blessed us;
let all the ends of the earth fear him!

The PROMISE *of* BLESSING

May God be gracious to us and bless us
and make his face to shine upon us.

A REFLECTION

When a child does something wrong they often go off and hide. I remember as a small child playing with matches and setting fire to a field of dry grass. My immediate reaction was to hide. And when I was eventually discovered I could not look my parents in the face. In the Genesis story, Adam and Eve are found hiding their faces from God. The inability to be face to face with someone speaks of broken friendship. Conversely, the image of two people looking at each other, face to face, speaks of openness and communion. It is a frequent biblical image. 'Thus the Lord used to speak to Moses face to face, as one speaks to a friend' (Exodus 33:11). The apostle Paul looked forward to the day when we all will see God 'face to face'. For, 'Now I know only in part; then I will know fully, even as I have been fully known' (1 Corinthians 13:12).

This prayer for God to make his face shine upon us is a prayer for communion with him. To begin to pray for this blessing is to turn our own faces, darkened with shame, back towards God. Communion with God is to look with face upturned into the shining face of God. Although he reels back in anger at the desecration of our lives, God is forever leaning forward smiling, giving himself to us in love and forgiveness. In this way he is true to his own nature and gracious to us. If we confess our sins, 'He who is faithful and just will forgive our sins and cleanse us from all unrighteousness' (1 John 1:9). It would be surprising if we did not need to rediscover this truth even today. Instead of finding ourselves head-bowed and shame-faced at the thought of God's presence, we can, on account of his gracious forgiveness, look up and with open face enjoy God's shining delight in us.

But this psalm has more than personal, individual blessing in mind. It is a prayer that God will bless the whole community. As we make it our own the 'us' will embrace home, church and the community at large. The blessings of God are experienced in both the provisions of nature and in God's intervention in history. These are his footprints as he makes his presence felt on the face of the earth. The psalm contains a surprising note of joy. It invites the nations to rejoice in the judgment of God. This may strike us as curious. How can sinners find joy in the thought of being judged by God? Of course, it is the fact that the judge is also a saviour and that his justice is plaited with compassion which makes joy possible for the sinner.

God is committed to righting the wrongs of the world. This is both a present and a future activity of God. When people reap what they sow, God is at the centre of this process exposing to people the truth of their actions. For example, the person who sows the seed of unrelenting selfishness reaps the consequence of loneliness. God exposes the essence of the action by the process of cause and effect in order to lead the person into a new way of thinking and living. This judgment is set to detonate an explosion of repentance. This is one aspect of the activity of God in righting the wrongs in the world. Yet anyone with even the slightest awareness of history and current affairs can see that this judgment of God *must* be more than a present activity. It must also belong to the future because so many wrongs still need to be righted and so much evil in the world goes unchallenged.

The Bible clearly points to a future experience of God decisively acting against all that is evil. There will be a final and climactic righting of all the wrongs in the universe. If this were not to be, the poor and the oppressed would justifiably rise up and wonder if the Lord were really a God of justice. As it is, the prophets, Jesus, and the New Testament all look forward to the day when God will establish a world of justice and 'judge the peoples with equity'.

A WORD *from* JESUS

Jesus said,

> 'You will see the Son of man seated at the right hand of Power, and coming with the clouds of heaven' (Mark 14:62).

A PRAYER

God of mercy, God of grace,
Show the brightness of thy face:
Shine upon us, Saviour, shine,
Fill thy Church with light divine;
And thy saving health extend
Unto earth's remotest end.

Let the people praise thee, Lord;
Be by all that live adored:
Let the nations shout and sing,
Glory to their Saviour King;
At thy feet their tributes pay,
And thy holy will obey.

Let the people praise thee, Lord;
Earth shall then her fruits afford;
God to man his blessings give,
Man to God devoted live;
All below, and all above,
One in joy, and light, and love.

Henry Francis Lyte, 1793–1847

CREATION RENEWED

PSALM 72:1–14, 17

Endow the king with your justice, O God,
the royal son with your righteousness.
He will judge your people in righteousness,
your afflicted ones with justice.
The mountains will bring prosperity to the people,
the hills the fruit of righteousness.
He will defend the afflicted among the people
and save the children of the needy;
he will crush the oppressor.

He will endure as long as the sun, as long as the moon,
through all generations.
He will be like rain falling on a mown field,
like showers watering the earth.
In his days the righteous will flourish;
prosperity will abound till the moon is no more.

He will rule from sea to sea
and from the River to the ends of the earth.
The desert tribes will bow before him
and his enemies will lick the dust.
The kings of Tarshish and of distant shores
will bring tribute to him;
the kings of Sheba and Seba
will present him gifts.
All kings will bow down to him
and all nations will serve him.

For he will deliver the needy who cry out,
the afflicted who have no one to help.
He will take pity on the weak and the needy
and save the needy from death.

He will rescue them from oppression and violence,
for precious is their blood in his sight.

The PROMISE of BLESSING

May his name endure for ever;
may it continue as long as the sun.
All nations will be blessed through him,
and they will call him blessed (Psalm 72:17).

A REFLECTION

St Edmund the martyr, king of East Anglia, took a year's sabbatical so that he could learn by heart every psalm! This was one of his favourites. Its ideals shaped his attitudes. It is a psalm that should be read, learned and inwardly digested by all who aspire to public office in local and national government—and by every voter.

This psalm inspires us with a picture of the ideal leader, the public servant. As the Jewish kings failed to live up to these expectations so the rays of light emanating from the psalm began to focus on the promised messiah. Although the New Testament never quotes these verses, the conclusion that Jesus, the Lord's anointed, captures in himself all the virtues of this public servant cannot be avoided.

When I first thought up the idea of this book I had a reservation that it might pander to an individualism and a personal piety that muted the call from God 'to do justice'. Trying to love God while ignoring our neighbour is as much a travesty of biblical faith as demanding justice for the oppressed without regard for that personal relationship of walking 'humbly with your God' (Micah 6:8). It is not either personal piety or social justice; it is both. And the psalter gives voice to this harmony. In this psalm we have a prayer that the leader will be endowed by God. The personal relationship between king and God is the source of his energetic defence of those in need.

William Wilberforce, one of the great public servants of the nineteenth century, struggled to redeem the lives of slaves 'from exploitation and outrage'. He exhausted himself to persuade the country and its leaders to abolish not only the slave trade but slavery itself. When, at the height of the struggle, Wilberforce was tempted to give up he received a letter from John Wesley. Wesley was the great evangelist who led thousands of men and women into a personal experience of the risen Christ. It was Wesley who encouraged Wilberforce to continue and to see that his political service and social reform were God's work too. Both personal evangelism and social reform belong to God's mission to renew his creation. One without the other is like trying to play a game of tennis with a swingball.

There is in this psalm an explicit imperialism. But the empire envisaged is not one of domination and exploitation. It is a kingdom where the claws of the oppressor have been removed, where the poor are guaranteed justice, where the life of every individual is deemed equally valuable.

This is the sort of world we should pray for; this is the quality of leadership we should covet. We must pray that the leaders of the world would take their cue from, and find their example in, Jesus who gives new stature and meaning to the office of public servant. Then shall we find blessing in and through him for the nations of the world.

A WORD *from* JESUS

Jesus read from the scriptures:

> 'The Spirit of the Lord is upon me,
> because he has anointed me to bring good news to the poor.
> He has sent me to proclaim release to the captives
> and recovery of sight to the blind,
> to let the oppressed go free,
> to proclaim the year of the Lord's favour' (Luke 4:18, 19).

Pray for the Spirit to anoint you.

MEDITATION *and* WORSHIP

Take the prayer of Jesus, 'Your kingdom come', and repeat it slowly. Make him king over your own interior life. Let his kingdom come first in you. This may lead you to confession and forgiveness.

Throughout this day as you work, walk, relax, find opportunities to repeat the prayer. Whenever you hear or see the news punctuate the bulletins with this silent prayer.

CALL *to* WORSHIP

PSALM 84:1—4

How lovely is thy dwelling place,
O Lord of hosts!
My soul longs, yea, faints
for the courts of the Lord:
my heart and flesh sing for joy
to the living God.

Even the sparrow finds a home,
and the swallow a nest for herself,
where she may lay her young,
at thy altars, O Lord of hosts,
my King and my God.
Blessed are those who dwell in thy house,
ever singing thy praise!

The PROMISE *of* BLESSING

Blessed are those who dwell in thy house,
ever singing thy praise.

A REFLECTION

I choose the opening verses of this psalm to read at the beginning of a service more than any other passage from the Bible. They hold before us a picture of a community of praise and so invite us to worship the Lord in the beauty of holiness.

The temple beckoned the pilgrim to worship. Yet their approach was very different from ours. Many of us when we go to church for a service cannot resist looking up the hymns before the service begins. Our hearts either sink or rise when we discover what hymns have been chosen. We find ourselves delighted to be singing a favourite hymn, only to be devastated when the organist beings to play the 'wrong' tune! What all this shows is that our attitude to worship is wrong. We have come to amuse ourselves. We have come to be entertained. So if the music is not to our liking we become irritated and leave the church like someone shortchanged by a mediocre concert.

This psalm reminds us who is to be the object of our worship: the living God. Christian worship is not for us to please ourselves. Worship is to please God. Singing hymns becomes an altogether different experience when we open the book and consciously address our songs of praise to God. Indulging in a healthy singalong is by comparison a very superficial religious experience. It may (when you get to sing all your favourite tunes) be enjoyable but it does not nourish spiritually.

I have been in gatherings when people have raised the roof with the great hymns of Newman and Wesley and have been in groups where people have sung the beautiful songs and choruses of Graham Kendrick. In both settings I have felt the music bind us together, and in that sense they have been religious experiences. But there was no worship. There were good feelings that came from singing good music, well composed and well sung. But there was no worship of God. The words were about God but our minds weren't focused on him. People had come to sing to please themselves. I have done it myself and even made the mistake of confusing the good feelings induced by such gatherings as blessings from God. You could argue that at least people had come together to praise God, and that this is very different from a rock or classical concert. Even so, true worship 'in spirit and in truth' must involve the heart and the mind.

We must come to 'the courts of the Lord' with a different attitude, with a different mind, with repentance. Think back to the last time you were in church. What was your attitude as you stood to sing the first hymn?

Let me suggest that the next time you are in church you could adopt these suggestions:

- Find the hymns and read them through before the service begins

- In the silence of your heart pray, 'I offer this praise to you, O living God'

- As you read silently, address the hymn to God

- When you stand to sing with the congregation, pray, 'I offer this praise to you, O living God'

This psalm gives us a picture of someone worshipping God with 'heart and flesh'. This means that his whole personality is involved—what we would call mind, emotion and will.

Mind

It is important that we know what we are saying about God and singing to him. Mindless worship is deficient: it can even be dangerous. Mindless worship can reinforce wrong ideas about God, and how he is at work in his world.

Emotion

We must be careful not to allow music to manipulate our emotions. But, at the same time we must allow the truth, grasped by our minds, that God loves us, to touch our emotions and move us. Worship that lacks emotion is also deficient. It can even be dangerous because emotionless worship can reinforce religious practice that is insensitive to the feelings of others.

Will

There will be many times when we do not feel like worshipping God. Our feelings can be affected by diet, sleep, time of the month, anxiety, lack of exercise. Such feelings are not to be trusted as the barometer of our relationship with God. When we don't feel like worshipping, that is when our will comes into play. 'No matter how I feel, I will worship you, O Lord.' It is remarkable that when we exercise the will to worship, the feelings can sometimes surge. But if we always wait for our feelings to ignite our soul to praise we will not be worshipping God very often. Worship that lacks the will simply does not happen.

The Bible reveals to us a God who delights in our worship. It is not because God needs it. He can exist without it just as a beautiful landscape will continue without anyone praising or painting it. God delights in our worship for in our worship we are at one with him. Just as a parent delights in the love of his children for in the warm embrace they are at one, so God, whose purpose from before Genesis to beyond Revelation is to reunite us all to himself, delights in every moment of union with his creation. Worship is to be at one with God. And herein lies the surprise. When we make God the object of our worship, when we sing praises not for ourselves but to the living God then we experience communion with God and 'at-one-ment' with him. And that is the blessing.

A WORD *from* JESUS

'But the hour is coming, and now is, when the true worshippers will worship the Father in spirit and truth, for such the Father seeks to worship him' (John 4:23).

A MEDITATION

The following spiritual exercise can be done anywhere and at any time (I first stumbled on the idea when lying in a hospital bed and unable to sleep in the early hours of the morning).

Using the alphabet as your guide, work through it as you worship God with a simple phrase. For example:

A   'I worship you O Lord for you are the **A**lmighty'

B   'I worship you O Lord for you promise to **B**less me'

C   'I worship you O Lord for your **C**ompassion'

D   'I worship you O Lord for you **D**etermine the course of creation'

Let your mind meditate on the picture that comes with the word that you choose. As soon as your mind begins to wander, move on to the next letter.

VALLEY *of* FEARS

PSALM 84:5—7

Blessed are those whose strength is in you,
who have set their hearts on pilgrimage.
As they pass through the Valley of Baca,
they make it a place of springs;
the autumn rains also cover it with pools.
They go from strength to strength,
till each appears before God in Zion.

The PROMISE *of* BLESSING

Blessed are those whose strength is in you,
who have set their hearts on pilgrimage.

A REFLECTION

The journey to the temple in Jerusalem was tedious and hazardous for pilgrims. The terrain was mountainous—muggers prowled at night. The pilgrims travelled in groups for safety: they kept their sights on their destination. The arduous physical journey to Jerusalem was a parable of the spiritual travelling that leads us to God. The route took pilgrims through the valley of dryness, the Vale of Baca, 'the Valley of Tears'. Yet paradoxically it is in this place of desolation that pilgrims intuit a meeting with God. It is like a spring of water that quenches the thirst of a weary traveller on a barren road, giving him or her strength to go on and complete the journey.

Two weeks after I had my appendix out, about fifteen years ago, I was rushed back to hospital on a Friday night with a piercing pain in my right lung and hardly able to breathe. I was admitted to a ward and then wheeled to the X-ray unit. After the radiographer had examined me he helped me back into the wheelchair and left me to be taken back to the ward by the porter. It was ten o'clock at night and the job of wheeling me back to my ward fell between two shifts. I was left on my own to wait. There seemed to me at that moment hardly a more desolate place on the face of the earth than this soulless and deserted X-ray unit. All I could hear were the distant echoes of a television down a long corridor. I couldn't shout out. It was too painful.

Yet as I sat in that wheelchair with a pulmonary embolism and everything conspiring against me I became unexpectedly and strangely aware of the presence of God. In particular, I sensed God speaking to me about the purpose of my life. My mind filled with the sound of an aria from Handel's *Messiah*; the words of the prophet Isaiah, 'How beautiful are the feet of them that preach the Gospel of peace', which I had heard sung on Christmas Day in my own church the previous month. The words gave meaning to my ministry and value to my life. I wasn't sure how much more of it I had to live but God had met with me in that valley of tears. As I sat in the abandoned wheelchair I *knew* that God was with me. In the cavernous corridor lined with empty seats God filled my heart with a desire to serve him. In that sterile atmosphere I was transfused with a life that had little to do with breathing. The porter duly arrived and rushed me back to the ward. I collapsed by the bed. Doctors and nurses were running. Curtains swirled around me. An injection immediately relieved the pain. I stayed awake all night, as 'high as a kite'. The weeks that followed the operation were filled with highs and lows. There were more tears than laughter but that encounter with the living God renewed my strength.

In moments of abject weakness we are thrown on to God. It is not success that drives us to God. More often than not it is success that entices us away from him. Weakness exposes us to God in a unique way and this is what the apostle Paul experienced: it is human weakness that opens up the gates to the energy of God. The Lord said so to Paul: 'My grace is sufficient for you, for power is made perfect in weakness'. Paul, who in spite of his achievements was no stranger to pain and suffering, responded: 'I will boast all the more gladly of my weaknesses, so that the power of Christ may dwell in me. Therefore I am content with weaknesses... for whenever I am weak, then I am strong' (2 Corinthians 12:9,10).

Therefore, as we journey to Jerusalem, to sing the praises of the living God, let us learn to value the Valley of Tears. In our weakness we can find his strength and blessing.

A WORD *from* JESUS

'Come to me, all you that are weary and are carrying heavy burdens, and I will give you rest' (Matthew 11:28).

A MEDITATION

Recall or imagine a mountainous landscape. Look carefully as if through binoculars at the mountain tops and in the valleys. What do you see? Do you notice that on the peaks of the mountains nothing grows and only in the valleys do the good things grow?

Review the last twelve months of your life. How would you describe them? Identify the valley and mountain-top experiences. What have you learned from being in the valley? What good things have begun to grow there as a result?

In a FOREIGN LAND

PSALM 84:8–12

O Lord God of hosts, hear my prayer:
give ear O God of Jacob.
Behold O God him who reigns over us:
and look upon the face of your anointed.

One day in your courts is better than a thousand:
I would rather stand at the threshold of the house of my God
than dwell in the tents of ungodliness.

For the Lord God is a rampart and a shield
the Lord gives favour and honour:
and no good thing will he withhold
from those who walk in innocence.
O Lord God of hosts:
blessed is the man who puts his trust in you.

The PROMISE *of* BLESSING

O Lord God of hosts:
blessed is the man who puts his trust in you.

A REFLECTION

The writer of this song seems to come from a country abroad ('One day in your courts is better than a thousand... in the tents of ungodliness'). The pilgrim has journeyed to the temple and now faces the prospect of returning to another country where the values and aspirations of the culture are so different from those of the Kingdom of God.

For a number of years when I was a teenager, my family lived in Singapore. It occurred to me that the further away you went from your native country the more patriotic and nationalistic you became. The singing of the national anthem by an expatriate community in a foreign land is always more fervent and intense than by the same people on their own soil! So it was with the Jewish people who lived beyond the borders. The thought of the temple and the singing of those songs bound them together, gave them a sense of identity and distinguished them from the people around. Their songs held before them a vision of uncluttered communion with God and inspired them to a life of devotion. The foreign land was full of seductive diversions but their worship of God reinforced their allegiance to the God of Jacob.

The plight of the pilgrim lamenting in a foreign land has resonances for the Christian conscious that he, too, is in some sense a stranger in this world. As the writer to Jewish Christians later observed: 'For here we have no lasting city, but we are looking for the city that is to come' (Hebrews 13:14). Like the pilgrim on his way down from the heights of Jerusalem who needs the protection of God as he engages with the world around, so we need the same armour of God: 'The Lord God is a rampart and shield.' These are defensive, not offensive weapons. They assume that the aggression is from another source. They speak of the conflict that every Christian is engaged in by virtue of his allegiance to Jesus Christ.

As we follow Jesus Christ and walk with God we will often find ourselves swimming against the tide. The secretary who is told by the boss to lie about his movements and refuses; the accountant who is told to falsify the accounts and resigns; the council worker who blows the whistle on malpractice and ends up getting the sack; the executive who is pressurized by colleagues to exaggerate his expenses and risks hostility by being honest; the manager who values people more than profits in a company that values profits more than people, and forfeits promotion. The straight and narrow path runs in the opposite direction and straight through the broad road that leads to the destruction of health, family, society and soul.

In these situations we need the protection of God. But what needs protecting is not 'us'. The Bible and Christian experience make it very clear that there is no protection from pain guaranteed. Look at Jesus on the cross. Consider the apostle Paul; how he was imprisoned, lashed, whipped, shipwrecked, robbed, betrayed, hungry, destitute and executed. There was no protection from pain for Jesus or for his disciples. What God promises to protect is *our relationship with him*, so that in and through our most difficult and troublesome moments 'we might evermore dwell in him and he in us'. So that with Paul we might also know that 'nothing can separate us from his love'; not even 'trouble, or hardship or persecution or hunger or poverty or danger of death'. Nothing can separate us from the love of God in Jesus Christ. That is the protection that God secures for us. God will not allow any disaster to sever his relationship with us and our relationship with him.

Nothing will stop God giving us his grace and favour. The one 'good thing' that the Lord will never withhold is his presence with us. In times of adversity when we are specially conscious of being at odds with the world for Christ's sake we will throw ourselves into the arms of God and trust ourselves to him. He is there. He is here. Such communion with the Lord of hosts is a blessing.

A WORD *from* JESUS

'Holy Father, protect them in your name... I am not asking you to take them out of the world, but I ask you to protect them from the evil one... As you, Father, are in me and I am in you, may they also be in us' (John 17:11, 15, 21).

Jesus prays for our protection, that no evil will ever get in the way of our relationship with God.

A PRAYER

Safe in the shadow of the Lord,
beneath his hand and power,
I trust in him,
I trust in him,
my fortress and my tower.

My hope is set on God alone
though Satan spreads his snare;
I trust in him,
I trust in him,
to keep me in his care.

From fears and phantoms of the night,
from foes about my way,
I trust in him,
I trust in him,
by darkness as by day.

His holy angels keep my feet
secure from every stone;
I trust in him,
I trust in him,
and unafraid go on.

Strong in the Everlasting Name,
and in my Father's care,
I trust in him,
I trust in him,
who hears and answers prayer.

Safe in the shadow of the Lord,
possessed by love divine,
I trust in him,
I trust in him,
and meet his love with mine.

Timothy Dudley-Smith

The COST *of* OBEDIENCE

The FACT *of* SUFFERING

PSALM 89:11–18

The heavens are thine, the earth also is thine;
the world and all that is in it, thou hast founded them.
The north and the south, thou hast created them;
Tabor and Hermon joyously praise thy name.
Thou hast a mighty arm;
strong is thy hand, high thy right hand.
Righteousness and justice are the foundations of thy throne;
steadfast love and faithfulness go before thee.
Blessed are the people who know the festal shout,
who walk, O Lord, in the light of thy countenance,
who exult in thy name all the day,
and extol thy righteousness.
For thou art the glory of their strength;
by thy favour our horn is exalted.
For our shield belongs to the Lord,
our king to the Holy One of Israel.

The PROMISE *of* BLESSING

Blessed are the people who know the festal shout,
who walk, O lord, in the light of thy countenance.

A REFLECTION

This extract does not give us the full flavour of this long psalm which is a lament. The cry is familiar: how can God allow suffering? The dilemma for the Jew was how could God, in the face of all his assurance of love, stand by and see his people suffer humiliation, pain and death?

With the coming of Jesus Christ into the world the light of God's countenance shines more fully: we see more clearly the true character of God. As we walk in the light, more aware of the nature of God, we begin to see the dilemma of divine love and human suffering in a different way. There are no easy answers, but there is a new way of looking at the problem.

Suffering is a fact of human existence, but it becomes especially problematic when you believe that there is a God who loves the world. When that faith is inspired by Jesus Christ then we can discover these unique insights.

The suffering God

Firstly, God is not a spectator of human suffering. In Jesus we meet the God who cries and suffers pain. He knows what it is like for us to suffer—he even bleeds like us. God suffers. The imagined division between a God of love remote in paradise and the human family enduring pain is a false one. Between the Garden of Eden and the Garden of Gethsemane God shows himself to the human family as one acquainted with grief. He knows what it is to be despised and rejected and to suffer pain. On the cross at Calvary he endured the physical pain of crucifixion, the emotional turmoil and loneliness of one who dies, and the spiritual desolation of separation from God the Father. God is no stranger to our suffering.

The eternal God

Secondly, Jesus sets the life of each of us in the context of eternity. His resurrection points to a reality greater than the one we now enjoy. This greater reality—heaven—offers a new perspective on this life, inviting us to keep a sense of proportion about all that befalls us. The New Testament teaching about our life after death gives Christians a clear perspective which may be summed up in six words: suffering is temporary, joy is eternal. If only we could renew our minds and discipline ourselves to see the world through the eyes of God (that is why Bible reading is so vital) then we would see that evil, suffering and death are not the last word on human life. I am not suggesting the mouthing of pious platitudes to people in pain but I am encouraging myself and all disciples of Jesus to break out of the contemporary mould of reacting to calamities and disasters as if we lived for this life only. It was because of the joy that was set before him that Jesus was enabled to endure the cross (Hebrews 12:2). The eternal dimension gave a context to his life: heaven sustained him in his moments of lonely agony. He was able to come to terms with his suffering because he lived in the light of the truth that God is eternal and suffering temporal.

The sovereign God

Thirdly, Jesus hints and the New Testament suggests that in some mysterious way God takes the suffering and weaves it into his glorious purpose for the healing of his creation. The classic example of this is the betrayal by Judas. Here was an act, inspired by the darkest power yet freely chosen, which God used to secure the salvation of the world. Such is the sovereign power of God he is able to turn our tragedies into triumphs. This truth invites us to discover in every bad deed the seed of something good.

I remember all too clearly when I had to take my eldest daughter, then aged four, to have some teeth extracted. This was the second occasion. On the first occasion she didn't know what was to happen and the moment she was injected in one of the arms that were embracing me she fell asleep. This time, though, she was quite aware of all that was happening. We entered the operating theatre, her face full of fear. She held on to me tightly, her arms clasped around my neck. She cried pitifully as the anaesthetist pressed the syringe into her arm. The injection had no effect and she cried with her head buried in my chest. In the end I had to lie on the bed with her, holding down her thrashing arms while the doctor held the mask over her struggling face until she breathed enough gas and collapsed into sleep. It was one of the most awful moments of my life. How I wish I could have taken her place and spared her the agony. I left the operating theatre drained and anxious. At one moment in the whole sickening process I was tempted to grab my daughter and run out of the theatre. But because I could see this moment of pain in the context of her whole life and that in this suffering lay the seed of goodness, the securing of her own welfare, I accepted it. I did not welcome it but I could come to terms with it. It is with similar perspectives that the Bible encourages the Christian to live with suffering and pain.

We are encouraged to walk today in the light of God's countenance. Because of Jesus we have more light than the psalmist. We have the light of God that shines in the face of Jesus Christ (2 Corinthians 4:6). In him we see the suffering God, the Eternal God, the Sovereign God. To know God means that, even in suffering, there is blessing.

A WORD *from* JESUS

In the Book of Revelation the voice from the throne of heaven says:

> 'God will wipe every tear from their eyes. Death will be no more; mourning and crying and pain will be no more, for the first things have passed away' (Revelation 21:4).

Suffering is temporary; joy eternal.

A MEDITATION

Recall a time of personal suffering. Describe it to yourself as if you were telling a friend. Imagine these things happening to Jesus. Describe the events to yourself.

The Sheltering God

Psalm 91:1–13, 15, 16

He who dwells in the shelter of the Most High
will rest in the shadow of the Almighty.
I will say of the Lord, 'He is my refuge and my fortress,
my God, in whom I trust.'

Surely he will save you from the fowler's snare
and from the deadly pestilence.
He will cover you with his feathers,
and under his wings you will find refuge;
his faithfulness will be your shield and rampart.
You will not fear the terror of night,
nor the arrow that flies by day,
nor the pestilence that stalks in the darkness,
nor the plague that destroys at midday.
A thousand may fall at your side,
ten thousand at your right hand,
but it will not come near you.
You will only observe with your eyes
and see the punishment of the wicked.

If you make the Most High your dwelling—
even the Lord, who is my refuge—
then no harm will befall you,
no disaster will come near your tent.
For he will command his angels concerning you
to guard you in all your ways;
they will lift you up in their hands,
so that you will not strike your foot against a stone.
You will tread upon the lion and the cobra;
you will trample the great lion and the serpent.

The PROMISE of BLESSING

'When he calls upon me I will answer him:
I will be with him in trouble
I will rescue him and bring him to honour.
With long life I will satisfy him:
and fill him with salvation' (Psalm 91:15, 16)

A REFLECTION

Although there is no explicit mention of blessing in this psalm it
is included by scholars in the psalms of blessing. It is easy to see
why, but it is difficult to apply these promises to a world where
suffering is ever present and bad things constantly happen to good
people. And it is worth reflecting that Satan tempted Jesus in the
wilderness with verses from this beautifully poetic psalm.

In Luke 4 we see the Spirit-filled Jesus directed by the Spirit of
God into the wilderness. Here the Son of God personally encounters the devil, the one who throws everything he can lay his hands
on against God and his servants. The devil directs Jesus either in
his imagination or in reality to Jerusalem and to the temple. Here
he attempts to seduce him with the idea that if he were to jump
from the pinnacle the angels of God would rush to his help and
save him from death. It is commonly thought that when Jesus
rejected the suggestion he nevertheless knew that had he jumped
he would have been safe. But I want to offer another insight which
throws a different light on the events.

Jesus already knew that to be obedient to God in this life did
not insure you against danger and death. He knew more than the
psalmist. He knew that to do God's will may well lead you to
suffering and pain. When Jesus spurned the devil's glib quotation
from scripture he knew that if he were to fall from the temple he
might well be killed. Jesus knew that God did not guarantee
angelic protection in this life, not even for his own Son. This theological insight was important in preparing him for Gethsemane
and Calvary. No angels would rescue him from the cross. In fact,
when the angel does make an appearance in the garden it is not

to rescue the victim in the nick of time but to strengthen him for the painful task and bitter cup (Luke 22:43).

Jesus' refusal to take a verse out of context sets an example for the interpretation of scripture and of the psalm in particular. We must investigate the promises of the psalms in the light of Jesus' own teaching and life and with the help of the New Testament. What, for example, are we to make of the promise, 'with long life I will satisfy him' made to the one who makes the Lord his 'refuge' and 'the Most High' his habitation? You and I will know Christians whose lives are racked by disease and whose life-expectancy is very short. I remember visiting someone in the final throes of a terminal illness. Her body bore the marks of her disease. I read this psalm which I had preached from the previous Sunday. I had to strain forward to hear her response: 'But I don't want *long* life.' There was no self-pity: her radiant face laughed at the thought and she was filled with the energy of faith as she looked beyond her death. 'I want *eternal* life,' she smiled. Her testimony gave me a clue to understanding this psalm afresh.

Her habitation, her dwelling place was evident to all as being in the shelter of the Most High, under the shadow of the Almighty. More clearly than the psalmist she was able to identify this place as being 'in Jesus Christ'. As a student she had come to him and since then, with lapses like the rest of us, had lived by faith in him. She in Christ and Christ in her. She lived, moved and had her being with him. She was possessed by him and by grace possessed him. She was able to pray, '*My* refuge and *my* fortress; *my* God, in whom I trust.' Through being in him she did not fear the condemnation of God of her sins; on the contrary, she found that glorious freedom that comes through Christ's unique forgiveness (Romans 8). Through being in union with him the life of God had already begun to flow to her. Because God is eternal his life is everlasting. That life eternal was already hers.

Physical death is powerless in staunching the flow of eternal life. Eternal life is not something we inherit beyond the grave but begins in us the moment we open ourselves to the gift of God and dwell in him. What the short-sighted psalmist saw as 'long life' the Christian sees with the spectacles of the New Testament as 'eternal life'. As we come to Christ and live by faith in him so we are transfused by the life of God. This life has its source in God and is, by definition, not just long but everlasting. That is why John wrote, 'God gave us *eternal* life, and this life is in his Son' (1 John 5:11). This is salvation and blessing in all their fullness.

A WORD *from* JESUS

'Those who drink of the water that I will give them will never be thirsty. The water that I will give will become in them a spring of water gushing up to eternal life.'

The woman said to him, 'Sir, give me this water' (John 4: 14–15).

PRAYER

Lord, fill me with your life.

JUSTICE & MERCY

PSALM 94:1–12

O Lord God to whom vengeance belongs:
O God to whom vengeance belongs, shine out in glory.
Arise, judge of the earth:
and requite the proud as they deserve.
Lord how long shall the wicked:
how long shall the wicked triumph?

How long shall all evildoers pour out words:
how long shall they boast and flaunt themselves?
They crush your people, O Lord:
they oppress your own possession.
They murder the widow and the alien:
they put the fatherless to death.
And they say, 'The Lord does not see:
nor does the God of Jacob consider it.'

Consider this you senseless among the people:
fools, when will you understand?
He who planted the ear does he not hear:
he who formed the eye does he not see?
He who disciplines the nations will he not punish:
has the teacher of mankind no knowledge?
The Lord knows the thoughts of man:
he knows that they are mere breath.

The PROMISE of BLESSING

Blessed is the person you discipline, O Lord (94:12).

A REFLECTION

I once had cause to scold one of my children, who was then aged about five. She ran up the stairs, threw herself on the carpet and shouted: 'Nobody loves me. Daddy doesn't love me; Mummy doesn't love me; Harriet doesn't love me; Tabitha doesn't love me.' As I listened to this litany of rejection I was beginning to have second thoughts about the severity of my rebuke! Then there was a pause followed by a final outburst: 'Only I love myself.' I was relieved to hear this massive vote of confidence in herself! The child is always tempted to interpret every severe experience as a sign of lovelessness and the child in every adult is also tempted to think that every difficult experience in life is a sign of God's lack of favour toward him. When problems arise people often feel that God must hate them and be punishing them for some misdemeanour or other. The disciple of Jesus who is maturing spiritually is beginning to see with the psalmist that God corrects and disciplines us not because he hates us but because he loves us. A good parent corrects his children because he loves them and wants the best for them. That is the source of God's discipline: love. Love cannot remain indifferent to the things that harm. Love must act against all that conflicts with what is good. That is in essence God's justice and judgment. It is not vindictive but is the just and right movement of God's spirit against all that is evil in favour of all that is good.

God is at work in his world raising up men and women to act against all that spoils his creation through tyranny and greed. That is the course of justice. The divine justice is blended with compassion and what ought to distinguish the Christian's cry for justice from that of others is an equal emphasis on forgiveness. The Kingdom of God has two cornerstones—justice and mercy.

But God is also at work in us individually. He moves against us at times, from our perspective disturbing us, frustrating us, and placing obstacles in our path. Sometimes he lets us taste the bitter fruit of our own choices. He is disciplining us, purging us of our ungodly ambitions, and stimulating in us an appetite for goodness—all because he loves us. This sort of correction and the processes involved are never pleasant. They are in my experience always painful. But, as the writer to the Hebrew Christians advised, they do ultimately yield 'the peaceful fruit of righteousness to those who have been trained by it' (Hebrews 12:11).

In Isaiah 5 God responds to the evils perpetrated by Israel in Jerusalem. In the Song of the Vineyard he threatens to leave the vineyard alone:

> *I will make it a waste;*
> *it shall not be pruned or hoed,*
> *and it shall be overgrown with briers and thorns' (Isaiah 5:6).*

The ultimate disaster for anybody is to be neglected by God; to be left to their own devices; to reap what they sow and to await the final judgment that is ushered in at the end of time. The present blessing that we should seek is to be attended to by God. His attention to our welfare, you will recall from Jesus' teaching about the vineyard, will mean frequent pruning of the branches. Such pruning is a sign of God's favour, both as individuals and as the church community. It is indicative of God's working with us, his attention and correction. This pruning and discipline are not to be feared and resisted, or to be interpreted as acts of divine lovelessness. On the contrary, we should be concerned if the marks of such pruning are absent from our lives. Times of uncertainty, disappointed ambitions, enforced patience and periods of loneliness can be acts of God in our lives to teach us greater dependence on him. To be neglected and abandoned by God would be a fate worse than death. To be disciplined by God means to be loved by him and therefore to be blessed by him.

A WORD *from* JESUS

'Every branch that bears fruit he prunes to make it bear more fruit' (John 15:2).

A MEDITATION

Picture in your mind a rosebush or a vine. Imagine one carefully tended and pruned where the branches are short. Imagine another where the branches have grown wild. See the two side by side.

In your imagination stand by the fruitless tree that is unpruned. Give names to the branches—immorality, lust, superstition, bitterness, conflict, jealousy, unjust anger, selfish ambition, rivalry, envy. Now allow God to prune these branches.

In your imagination stand by the tree that is pruned. Give names to the abundant flowers and fruit—self-control, gentleness, faithfulness, goodness, kindness, patience, peace, joy and love.

Ask the Father to enable you by the Spirit of Jesus to bear much of this fruit and yield to his pruning work.

Read Galatians 5:16–25 and John 15.

Proclaim *the* Healing

Psalm 106:1–5

Praise the Lord.
O give thanks to the Lord for he is good:
and his mercy endures for ever.
Who can express the mighty acts of the Lord:
or fully voice his praise?
Blessed are those who act according to justice:
who at all times do the right.

Remember me, O Lord
when you visit your people with favour:
and come to me also with your salvation,
that I may see the prosperity of your chosen:
that I may rejoice with the rejoicing of your people
and exult with those who are your own.

The Promise of Blessing

Blessed are those who act according to justice:
who at all times do the right.

A Reflection

This psalm opens with a ringing declaration about the character of
God. It is the prelude to a prayer for forgiveness which confesses
the sins not of an individual but of the nation. If you read to the
end of the psalm you will find a catalogue of evil that eroded
national life.

Because our society is structured differently from that of the
Old Testament (ours a democracy, theirs a theocracy) the application of this psalm to our own national situation may be doubted.
But I want to make two points, firstly about the role of the church
in a nation's life and secondly about the relationship of the

character of God to human behaviour and ethics.

These communal psalms of confession were led by the priests and the Levites. The Levites recited the sins of all the people. They led the congregation in seeking the forgiveness of God for their misdemeanours, past and present. And at the altar it was the priest who, through the offering of a sacrifice, interceded for the people and secured forgiveness from the God of justice and mercy. The role of the priests and the Levites in the life of the nation may give a model to the church of her own role in national life. In the first letter of Peter, the followers of Jesus Christ are styled as a 'holy priesthood, to offer spiritual sacrifices acceptable to God through Jesus Christ'. Those who received the mercy of God are characterized as a 'royal priesthood' who are called to 'proclaim the mighty acts of him who called you out of darkness into his marvellous light' (1 Peter 2:4–10). This was exactly the priestly function of the Levites in the Old Testament: to declare the deeds of Yahweh to his people and to offer sacrifices on behalf of all the people.

The Church constitutes the new priesthood. But it is the priesthood firmly rooted and earthed in the world with a ministry to that wider community which Peter summarizes as 'Honour everyone. Love the family of believers. Fear God. Honour the emperor' (1 Peter 2:17). The priestly ministry of the Church is to proclaim to the world the healing works of God and to lead the world in confession of its sins. This is why in the liturgy of our churches at the moment of confession it is appropriate for Christians to identify themselves with social, national and international injustices, for, like the priests of the Old Testament, we are seeking forgiveness not just for our own involvement in these sins but on behalf of the world. That is the thrust of the Church praying that God would have mercy on the world. Just as the priest bridged the gulf between Yahweh and his people so the Church, through both its evangelistic and sacramental ministry, stands as a bridge between God and the world he loves.

The promise of blessing in this psalm is to those who 'do the right'. Justice is seen not as something you discuss. Justice is to be done: 'Do justice.' To act justly is to reflect the very character of God. Therefore it is incumbent on every Christian to examine their actions and relationships and to ask if they are being fair and just in their dealings. Much has been written on the theme of justice, to the point that the word is in danger of falling on to the scrap-heap of religious clichés. In order to avoid hastening such a destiny let me go off at what at first appears as a tangent!

In the Bible the justice of God is always balanced by an emphasis on his mercy. For example, the psalm reminds us of the victory of justice and of the goodness of God's character but adds that his 'mercy endures for ever'. Justice and mercy present a fuller revelation of the nature of God than does the singular emphasis upon his justice. This is vitally important. There can be such an obsession in the human personality with righteousness and justice that people become graceless and unforgiving. History and contemporary life provide countless examples of such people who, either in the field of personal morality or social justice, have become rigid in their demands and unforgiving of those who have erred. Sadly, such people are also and often to be found in the Church. We have to remind ourselves that the biblical vision of God is the God of justice *and* mercy and that the community that has been called out of darkness into light must reflect not only his righteousness but also his grace.

Jesus encountered the same difficulty. The Pharisees were, by and large, sticklers for the rules. They clearly defined and knew what was right and wrong. But, as the gospels and contemporary Jewish literature reveal, they lacked the grace to accommodate the detractor. When, for example, Jesus healed on the Sabbath or associated with a prostitute they were outraged. Perhaps they confused compassion with compromise or felt their security threatened by the apparent undermining of their meticulous rules. Whatever the social or psychological reasons for their obsession with 'doing the right thing', Jesus challenges the attitudes of the Pharisees: 'Unless your righteousness exceeds that of the scribes and Pharisees, you will never enter the Kingdom of Heaven.' On first reading, this may sound dreadful. Is Jesus seriously asking us to be even more meticulous than the Pharisees in defining and sticking to the rules? What could this 'righteousness' be that exceeds that of the Pharisees? Well, righteousness that exceeds and surpasses that of the Pharisees is a righteousness that is accompanied by grace, a justice that is blended with mercy. This is what the graceless Pharisees lacked. And this is what so many Christians lack too—mercy and grace. Such an understanding makes sense of the complete statement: 'Unless your righteousness exceeds that of the scribes, you will never enter the Kingdom of Heaven.' What secures our entry to heaven is not our righteousness but God's mercy.

It is divine mercy, personally experienced by us and evident in our lives, that is to accompany our passion for righteousness and justice. God save us from radicals who speak only of justice and from moralists who talk only of righteousness. God make us men and women who love mercy as well as acting justly. This is what it means to walk humbly with the God of justice and mercy (see again Micah 6). Blessing will flow to such walkers from the God who is 'good' and whose 'mercy endures for ever'.

A WORD *from* JESUS

Jesus said,

'Blessed are those who hunger and thirst for righteousness, for they shall be satisfied. Blessed are the merciful, for they shall obtain mercy' (*Matthew 5:6, 7*).

These two verses should be remembered together.

A MEDITATION

Lord save me from being a radical who knows no mercy;
from being a moralist who knows no compassion.
Make me a lover of mercy in your passion for justice.

Consider now those people whom you feel are in the wrong or have done something wrong. How far does your attitude reflect the mercy as well as the justice of God?

Pray that God would have mercy on a merciless world.

Lord have mercy.
Christ have mercy.
Lord have mercy.

FEAR & JOY

PSALM 112:1–10

Hallelujah!
Blessed is the man who fears the Lord,
who greatly delights in his commandments!
His descendants will be mighty in the land;
the generations of the godly will be blessed.
Wealth and riches are in his house;
and his righteousness endures for ever.
To those who fear God he is like a light that shines in darkness:
he is merciful, gracious and righteous.
It is well with the man who is merciful and lends;
he conducts his affairs with justice,
for he will never be moved;
the righteous will be remembered for ever.
He is not afraid of evil rumours;
his heart is firm, trusting in the Lord.
His heart is confident,
he is afraid of nothing,
so that he can (calmly) watch his enemies.
He has given generously to the poor;
his righteousness is established for ever;
his horn is exalted in honour.
The wicked man sees it and is angry;
he is dismayed and gnashes his teeth;
the desire of the wicked comes to nought.

The PROMISE of BLESSING

Blessed is the man who fears the Lord,
who greatly delights in his commandments!

A REFLECTION

What is the most frequent command in the Bible? Love God? Love your neighbour? The most repeated order is 'Fear the Lord.' The second most popular command is 'Rejoice.' Obedience to these two commands is reflected in this promise of blessing to those who both fear the Lord and who enjoy and rejoice in God's commandments. Fear and joy are coupled together as the hallmarks of persons in communion with God. At first one may appear the antithesis of the other.

Fear

This fear is not the same as being frightened. It is not a destructive fear that closes the person up and renders them incapable of moving forward. It is not like the fear of a child frightened by going to a new school. It is not the fear of an adult frightened by the thought of being rejected. It is not like a phobia that induces paralysing panic and irrational responses. These fears are negative. The fear of God is positive. The fear of the Lord is healthy and life-giving. Instead of closing you up to the source of the fear, the fear of the Lord opens you up to the vital possibilities of a relationship with God.

It is difficult to find a suitable word to render the meaning of fear when applied to God.

Imagine standing by a great waterfall. Imagine thousands of tons of mountain water thundering downwards: the relentless power, the incessant and deafening roar, the inexorable spray saturating every spectator with an awesome awareness of the sheer and voluminous greatness of this fall of water. And in the presence of such power comes a feeling of your own smallness. But the sight of such power is exhilarating. Although part of you would hold back for the sake of safety, another part is drawn to the edge, to feel the spray on your face, to smile, to breathe deeply as if to quench your thirst in the purifying goodness of these powerful waters. There is nothing static about the awe of this moment. The source of the awe possesses a compelling attraction. In a not altogether dissimilar way, the awe of God does not repel but draws us into himself.

The analogy of the waterfall, although helpful, is ultimately inadequate for it is essentially impersonal. Our fear of God is a response not just to the power of God, for which the waterfall is an appropriate analogy, but to the love of God which is personal. In the Bible the fear of the Lord is the right expression that follows the vivid impression that his love makes upon our lives.

Some people say, 'God loves us. He can do nothing else. That's his nature.' Although I have said this myself and can see what people are driving at, namely, 'It is God's character to love,' I have some misgivings. If my wife told me that she loved me, that she could do nothing else but love me, that she was without personal decision in this matter and that she had no choice, I doubt that I would feel beloved. The mystery of love, indeed the joyful mystery, is that the lover *chooses* to love the beloved. The lover is not some automatic robot programmed to show expressions of kindness but is possessed of a freedom to choose to love and to set his love on whomever he wills to love. The mystery of my wife's love for me is that, given all that she knows about me, she nevertheless continues to choose to love me. This freedom and maturity characterizes the love of God. He chooses to love us, exercising the freedom that he has uniquely, and wills to love us.

This idea of 'choice in love' was especially revealed to the Jews in the Old Testament: God made it clear to them that he *chose* to set his love upon them (see Deuteronomy 7). They had no grand qualifications for being loved by God. God simply took the initiative and chose to love them. This important point is not only overlooked, but sometimes misconstrued. People come unstuck on the idea of God choosing and deduce that if God chose the Jews then he left the rest of the world unchosen. To hold this view flies in the face of the full biblical revelation that God chooses to love the *whole* world. The relation between God and the Jewish people is there as a parable in history of how God loves. And in particular, it reveals that at the heart of love there lies a freedom of choice. God opens our eyes to this truth by showing us that in his relationship with the Jews he chose to love them. This relationship is a paradigm of all the relationships initiated by God. God chose to love the Jews not because they deserved it but because he willed it. And so in our relationship with God we discover that he loves us, not because we deserve it, not because he is incapable of not loving us, but because he chose to love us. When we see truthfully into our own lives we may well marvel that God should so choose. Yet this is the Gospel, that God so loves the world and that while we were yet sinners God gave Christ to die for us. Such love draws from the beloved a sense of awe. It evokes from us a 'fear' that draws us nearer to enquire further about the nature of this love, that opens us up to the healing properties of God's love, that astonishes us that we should ever be the beloved of God. This is why blessing belongs to the one who has come to fear the Lord for his power and love.

Rejoice

If at first joy and fear seemed odd bedfellows, maybe now they do not appear to be such strangers to each other. The power and love of God induce in us an inner smile. Hopefully you have already begun to respond positively to the miracle of God wilfully choosing to love *you*. The joy that flows from such an experience has a particular focus in this psalm. The great biblical commandments are not simply laws so as to keep a semi-nomadic community together; they are expressions of the character of God—his passionate attachment to all that is just, his setting his face against all that diminishes and destroys the glory of creation. Being conversant with and living in obedience to the commandments of God is the path to knowing God more clearly. The Law mediates his character and purpose and, as Paul later expounded, exposes our own deviations from his goodness. We are to cherish and rejoice in the Law of God because of these two ministries. Firstly, it reveals to us the glorious character of God. Secondly, it reveals to us our own need of the grace and forgiveness of God which are so generously forthcoming.

A WORD *from* JESUS

Jesus said to his disciples,

> *'If you love me, you will keep my commandments. And I will ask the Father, and he will give you another Advocate, to be with you for ever. This is the Spirit of truth…' (John 14:15–16)*

A PRAYER

May the mind of Christ my Saviour
Live in me from day to day,
By his love and power controlling
All I do and say.

May the Word of God dwell richly
In my heart from hour to hour,
So that all may see I triumph
Only through his power.

Kate Wilkinson, 1859–1928

ETERNAL PERSPECTIVES

PSALM 112:1–10

O praise the Lord.
Blessed is the man who fears the Lord:
and greatly delights in his commandments.
His children shall be mighty in the land:
a race of upright men who will be blessed.
Riches and plenty shall be in his house:
and his righteousness stands for ever.
Light arises in darkness for the upright:
gracious and merciful is the righteous man.
It goes well with the man who acts generously and lends:
who guides his affairs with justice.
Surely he shall never be moved:
the righteous shall be held in everlasting remembrance.
He will not fear bad tidings:
his heart is steadfast, trusting in the Lord.
His heart is confident and will not fear:
he will see the downfall of his enemies.
He gives freely to the poor:
his righteousness stand for ever
his head is uplifted in glory.
The wicked man shall see it and be angry:
he shall gnash his teeth and consume away
and the hope of the wicked shall fail.

The PROMISE of BLESSING

His children shall be mighty in the land:
a race of upright men who will be blessed.

This psalm promises a vindication of those who conduct their affairs with justice. It envisages parents who fear the Lord and delight in his commandments, giving birth to a family who in turn will cherish the ideals of their parents. It recognizes that the virtuous will encounter opposition and misrepresentation, and anticipates a dark and negative climate. In these respects, the psalm is utterly realistic about the difficulties of keeping to the straight and narrow path. For those without an inkling of eternal life this psalm would lead them to believe that the material vindication of the just would always happen on this side of the grave. Indeed, the author of this psalm expresses such an expectation. But just as every poem has a life of its own after it has left the imagination and pen of its author, so this psalm evokes other images from the minds and hearts of those who have in their hearts fed on Jesus Christ. In particular, we know that love does not by any means conquer all in this life. The love of Jesus did not overcome his enemies. The power of Jesus did not ensure his not running into danger. The justice of Jesus did not ensure for him a fair trial. The integrity of Jesus did not triumph over the lies of his accusers. The compassion of Jesus did not soften the hearts of his accusers. From a human point of view, the day on which he died stands as a monumental disaster for all who hoped and continue to hope that truth and justice, love and peace will always ultimately succeed in this life. It is only the event of the resurrection that bestows on that Friday the epithet 'Good'. Without it that Sabbath eve is a holocaust, witnessing to the dark destruction of the one true, honourable, just, pure, lovely, gracious and excellent person ever to tread the verge of light and darkness. Only the resurrection of this true person nullifies our pessimism and sets our precarious existence in the continent of eternity. Here is the provenance of our optimism as Christians. The vindication of the just is God's work; we see shadows of it in this world (Romans 12:19—13:4) and savour poetic aspirations of it in psalms like this one but the completion of the vindication will be on another shore. Christians today are in danger of losing this eternal dimension because we are anxious to correct the false impression of offering people only 'pie in the sky when you die'. We eschew being 'so heavenly minded that we're of no earthly use'. But the result is that we are in peril of losing the eternal perspective altogether. And if we do, then we are prone to being demoralized, for the world gives no vast encouragement to virtue.

When I was working in Bristol at the start of my ministry in the Church of England, I overheard some young Christian graduates talking about giving up their careers in the professional caring services and going into business. The commercial venture was to provide nursing homes for the elderly which, as our elderly population is increasing dramatically, is already becoming big business. I am all for creating wealth, for adventure, for caring for the elderly, and I am open to this being a blend of private and community provision. What saddened me was the quality of the discussion and the consideration of 'the old people' as a means of making money for those budding entrepreneurs. Their values seemed no different from those of others who would express no allegiance to Jesus Christ. Their ambitions seemed as worldly as those of others who have neither awareness of nor aspiration to life eternal. It seems to me that our minds are being shaped more thoroughly by the world around than by the teachings of Christ. In the light of this psalm the elders must ask whether the children of the church 'will be mighty in the land', whether we are giving birth to and nurturing 'a race of upright men and women who will be blessed'.

This psalm, for all its short-sightedness about virtue being materially rewarded in this life, nevertheless gives us a portrait of the sort of people we should be shaping in the bosom of the church. Such a person is 'gracious and merciful', who 'guides his affairs with justice' and 'gives freely to the poor'. It is to such people that God promises blessing. It may seem that this is the reward for their goodness, and this idea may make us feel uncomfortable, for surely it is not ethical to do something good simply because there is a reward at the end. Certainly there is something questionable about saying to a young person, 'If you help that old lady across the road I'll give you a pound.' It is not immoral to do so but neither is it virtuous. If, however, I encourage a young person to learn the guitar because he will one day enjoy playing it, the reward belongs to the activity. He is not rewarded *for* playing it but *in* playing it. There is an appreciation and satisfaction at the heart of the experience: it belongs to the nature of the action. The reward that comes to the upright also belongs to the very activity of guiding one's affairs with justice. There is an appreciation and satisfaction at the heart of the experience of doing what is right. The more we learn to act justly and to love mercy, the more we live in tune with the rhythm of God's soul. Even when it is difficult to do this and to do so brings no material benefits, there is an inner rectitude that accompanies the actions of justice and mercy. Whether we call this attendant appreciation and satisfaction 'a natural outcome' or 'an inevitable consequence' or 'a reward', it is straightforwardly named by the psalmist and Jesus as a 'blessing'.

We need constantly to remind ourselves that doing the right thing has its own intrinsic value, worth and satisfaction, and to teach it to future generations. Blessed is the person who does what is right. Blessed even in this life and blessed for ever.

A WORD *from* JESUS

We have heard it many times before but we need to hear it again:

'Blessed are those who hunger and thirst for righteousness, for they will be filled' (Matthew 5:6).

A PRAYER

Lord give me the appetite
to do that which is right
and to be satisfied by doing
that which pleases you.

ELUSIVE HUMILITY

PSALM 115:1–11, 12–13

Not to us, O Lord, not to us,
but to thy name give glory,
for the sake of thy steadfast love and thy faithfulness!
Why should the nations say,
'Where is their God?'
Our God is in the heavens;
he does whatever he pleases.
Their idols are silver and gold,
the work of men's hands.
They have mouths, but do not speak;
eyes, but do not see.
They have ears, but do not hear;
noses, but do not smell.
They have hands, but do not feel;
feet, but do not walk;
and they do not make a sound in their throat.
Those who make them are like them;
so are all who trust in them.

O Israel, trust in the Lord!
He is their help and their shield.
O house of Aaron, put your trust in the Lord!
He is their help and their shield.
You who fear the Lord, trust in the Lord!
He is their help and their shield.

The PROMISE *of* BLESSING

The Lord has been mindful of us; he will bless us;
he will bless the house of Israel;
he will bless the house of Aaron;
he will bless those who fear the Lord,
both small and great (115:12, 13).

A REFLECTION

After the Battle of Agincourt, Henry V commanded all his men to kneel on the ground as the verse of this psalm rang out: *Non nobis, Domine, non nobis, sed nomini tuo da gloriam.* (Not to us, O Lord, not to us, but to thy name give glory.') Shakespeare immortalized the words in Henry's victory speech:

> *Do we all holy rites;*
> *let there be sung 'Non nobis' and 'Te Deum'.*

This is the prayer of humble men and women. This is the path of humility to seek glory not for ourselves but for God. But it is also a most unnatural act. Whether it is to do with our instinct to survive or with our psychological need for affirmation and security, or with the plain fact that we are flawed, we enjoy basking in the glory of our achievements. If it stopped at simple enjoyment and godly pride, there would not be such a problem. The truth is that we often scheme at gaining more glory than we deserve. We play down the part of others in our achievements; we throw away a word that diminishes the stature of others and elevates our own standing. The humble person is, by contrast, a supernatural creation. He or she is freed from that competitive urge to achieve status and its attendant glory, and is keen to pay tribute to the contributions of others to his or her own success. He or she acknowledges that the origins of their resourcefulness belongs elsewhere and delights in giving glory to God.

But how are we to attain such humility? How can we cut the self down to size? Humility is not only supernatural: it is an elusive virtue. The moment you try to be humble, the instant you begin to examine yourself for signs of humility, all hope of being humble vanishes. The essence of humility is self-effacement. The opposite of humility is self-obsession. It is as impossible to see humility in yourself as it is to look in a mirror and see yourself blinking.

This psalm, which begins with the prayer of humility, actually charts a path of humility. It was sung in their liturgy as the people of God came together to worship. The song not only expressed a humble approach to God but it also reinforced in their minds and hearts the means of remaining before God a humble community. The primary focus in the psalm is the steadfast love and faithfulness of God. The people had experienced this even in the face of doubts ('Where is their God?'). They were able to look back and see that against the odds God had kept them together. For example, he had rescued them from Egypt (see the previous psalm 114); the odds against them getting out and into the promised land were enormous. But God kept his promise and delivered them. These acts of God declared to his people that he loved them and would never abandon them. As a community they kept a record of their corporate spiritual journey which they continually rehearsed when they worshipped together. The psalm formed the diary of their spiritual journey. Just as some people today keep a diary that logs their spiritual journey, so the Jews did this in their psalms and songs of God's deliverance. It enables you to go back and remember how God has guided you, thereby giving you confidence and courage for the future. And more than this, such a record of God's love and faithfulness keeps you humble: by focusing on God and his achievements the self is properly neglected.

The Jewish community looked not only to its history but also to the heavens. This psalm shifts the poet's attention to celebrate the author of creation. 'Our God is in the heavens; he does whatever he pleases.' The contrast is made between the gods who were purely projections of human aspirations and the sovereign God of the universe. There is something almost cosmic about these silvery golden gods who are made in the image of man for they can't actually do even the basic human functions! In spite of their metallic glory these idolized gods are mute, blind, deaf, insensitive, and disabled. As such they allow men and women to get away with whatever they wish and indulge every fantasy. Such fabricated idols still exist today.

For many years now I have been involved in evangelism. In small group discussions and in personal conversations a certain phrase crops up with regularity. People talk about 'My God'. 'My god doesn't do that...', 'My god would...' The gods that they describe exist only in the realms of their imagination and solely as a projection of their own aspirations, allowing them to do whatever they want. Their gods have been fabricated in their image and after their likeness: it is they themselves who prescribe to their gods what is permissible. Such gods bear no resemblance to the sovereign God of heaven and earth who reveals himself in creation and history as the one God who sees, hears and speaks, and who in the person of Jesus Christ actually walked the earth, touching and feeling the pangs of human existence. By focusing on the God of heaven and earth a certain humility descends to clothe the spectator, not least his mind. When men and women live in the awesome awareness that it is God who stands at the centre and who does whatever he pleases, there is a proper neglect of self.

Whenever I am perplexed about something I have to confess that it is often because I see myself standing at the centre of the universe. Concern for myself grows out of all proportion. But I have learned (if only I did it naturally!) to take conscious steps to walk away from the centre and to make myself see God standing in the central space which I have vacated. The problems do not disappear but there is a peace that arises from dethroning the self and enthroning God. This is what the Jews were learning to do throughout their history.

For the Jews and for us the promise of blessing in this psalm is based upon the assurance that 'the Lord has been mindful of us'. Forgetfulness is not a characteristic of God. He remembers us. He cannot get us out of his mind. He does not want to get us out of his thoughts. God loves us with all his mind. This is why he will bless us: not because we are great and deserve his affection; not because we are small and need his attention; but because he chooses to think about us and to care for us—whoever we are. This is the love that stands at the centre of the universe and is the source of all blessing. Should we ever doubt this love then we have more cause than the psalmist to be reassured (his sense of God's love was strong even though he lacked the insights of the incarnation and eternity). Look at Jesus. God *so* loved us he gave us

Jesus (John 3:16). 'He who did not withhold his own Son, but gave him up for all of us, will he not with him also give us everything else?' (Romans 8:32). And when we look at Jesus not only shall we see how much he loves us but also we shall so fill our thoughts with his steadfast love and faithfulness that we too shall cry out: 'Not to us but to thy name give glory.' And at that moment something else shall happen!

A WORD *from* JESUS

'Consider the lilies of the field, how they grow; they neither toil nor spin; yet I tell you, even Solomon in all his glory was not clothed like one of these. But if God so clothes the grass of the field... will he not much more clothe you—you of little faith? Therefore do not worry...' (Matthew 6:28–31)

We can take comfort and reassurance from these words.

A MEDITATION

In your mind (or on paper) draw a circle around yourself. Around the circumference set all the affairs of your life. Allow yourself the time to feel any pressure or panic as you stand surrounded by these issues.

In your imagination see Jesus coming towards you. He kneels outside the circle and begins to roll up these affairs like a carpet. He carries the burden and walks towards you in the centre. You kneel. Hear the Father say:

'Cast all your anxieties on him, for he cares about you.'

In due course stand and say to him:

'Not to me but to you be the glory.'

RESTING *in* HIS PRESENCE

RESCUED

PSALM 118:1—9, 26—29

O give thanks to the Lord, for he is good;
his steadfast love endures for ever!

Let Israel say,
'His steadfast love endures for ever.'
Let the house of Aaron say,
'His steadfast love endures for ever.'
Let those who fear the Lord say,
'His steadfast love endures for ever.'

Out of my distress I called on the Lord;
the Lord answered me and set me free.
With the Lord on my side I do not fear.
What can man do to me?
The Lord is on my side to help me;
I shall look in triumph on those who hate me.
It is better to take refuge in the Lord
than to put confidence in man.
It is better to take refuge in the Lord
than to put confidence in princes…
Thou art my God, and I will give thanks to thee;
thou art my God, I will extol thee.

O give thanks to the Lord, for he is good;
for his steadfast love endures for ever!

The PROMISE *of* BLESSING

Blessed be he who enters in the name of the Lord!
We bless you from the house of the Lord.
The Lord is God, and he has given us light.
Bind the festal procession with branches, up to the horns of the altar.
(Psalm 118:26–27)

A REFLECTION

This was the favourite psalm of Martin Luther.

This is my psalm which I love—for truly it has deserved well of me many a time and has delivered me from many a sore affliction when neither emperor nor kings nor the wise nor the cunning nor the saints were able or willing to help me.

The psalm is shot through with a positive and joyful faith like concrete reinforced with steel rods. The faith is unshakeable: far from being undermined and weakened by adversity its resilient strength becomes all the more apparent in times of great trouble.

This psalm clearly belonged to the liturgy of the temple and shows the vibrancy of their worship. There is nothing muted or subdued here. If only our worship reflected the same joyful reverence! Blessing was promised to the people as they stood at the entrance of the temple sanctuary. 'Blessed be he who enters in the name of the Lord.' The priests pronounced the blessing over people who responded by dancing around the altar with festal garlands and branches of palms. The priestly blessing about God giving light echoed the benediction in Numbers 6:

The Lord spoke to Moses, saying: 'Speak to Aaron and his sons,
saying, thus you shall bless the Israelites:
The Lord bless you and keep you;
the Lord make his face to shine upon you, and be gracious to you;
the Lord lift up his countenance upon you, and give you peace.
So they shall put my name on the Israelites, and I will bless them'
(vv. 22–27).

It is difficult for us in this neon-lit world to imagine the dense darkness of a night without any light and to appreciate the significance of shining light as a metaphor of God's presence. I remember as an army cadet taking part in a military exercise one night on the Pennine Hills. The rest of my section was 'captured' but I escaped into some woods. The moon was shrouded in clouds and the night was very dark. I could see nothing; I lay low. But my smug satisfaction at escaping capture soon gave way to fear as I realized that I was now on my own in the hills. I called out, louder and louder, but was only met with silence. I tried to move out of the woods. Sheer terror gripped me as I stumbled into a sheep: I rushed forward and fell knee-high into a bog. I began to panic at the prospect of other dangers lurking in the darkness as I groped towards the edge of the wood. Then, all of a sudden, I heard the sound of a Landrover in the distance. Its headlights pierced the darkness. The vehicle swung round slowly, the beam of the lamps lighting up the landscape. I shouted and waved my arms furiously until the full strength of the Landrover's headlights rested on this exhausted, yet relieved, khaki-clad cadet. Seeing the light filled me with hope and assured me that I was no longer lost and alone. The light dispelled the dread, promising rescue and safety. The light gave me energy not only to walk but to run towards my rescuers who wrapped me in a blanket and plied me with hot, strong, sweet tea. The light had filled me with hope, relief, joy and weeping gratitude. I could see all that lay around me. I was safe.

The presence of God is a light that shines in darkness. Sometimes our personal worlds seem very dark places. We can feel hemmed in by the real and imagined dangers that lurk in the darkness. We are to remember, with the psalmist, that 'the Lord is God' and that by gracing our lives with his presence 'he has given us light'.

The temple worshippers became more and more aware of the divine presence as they drew nearer the sanctuary. At the heart of the temple was the Holy of Holies where the ark of the covenant stood. This symbolized the presence of God on earth. Communion with God in the temple, 'the home of the Lord', inspired in the worshipper a fresh awareness of God's grace: 'O give thanks to the Lord for he is good: for his steadfast love endures forever.' It was as if the nearer they got to the Holy of

Holies the more conscious they became of God. The focus of their attention shifted away from their own problems and on to the goodness and love of God. Their delight in God built up to an ecstatic crescendo. It was like a light that filled their minds and hearts. It banished the darkness within, flooding their whole being with light. Their problems did not go away: soon they would have to leave the temple and return to their difficult situations. But standing there in the house of the Lord, delighting in his goodness and love, was like being bathed in warm light. It was real. And it was here, in this moment of communion, that they found the energy and the strength to go on.

I find in this psalm an example and an encouragement to draw near to God and delight in his goodness and love. But, you may object, 'my life is too fraught with problems'. All the more reason for you to come into the sanctuary. You will find no peace in holding on to your problems. Abandon them for a moment; come to him and say, 'His steadfast love endures forever'; grit your teeth and brace your heart and say it again: 'His steadfast love endures forever.' Let the tears of darkness and doubt fill your eyes and say, 'His steadfast love endures forever.' Let the objections rise and subside as you say, 'His steadfast love endures forever.'

So the light of God will fill you: it is a genuine experience of God. It will humble you and lead you to confession. It will lead you to peace and to thanksgiving. The light of God spoke not only of God's presence but also of the quality of God's presence and of his character. To stand in the light of God means to become aware of his moral purity, the integrity of his dealings with us. Therefore, as we draw near so we marvel at the eager willingness of the Holy God to shine his light upon us and to bless us. He stoops down to lift up the humble, he faithfully forgives all those who confess their sins, he anoints and heals the brokenhearted, he breathes peace into our diseased souls and puts a new song into our hearts. The song is one of praise and thanksgiving and we sing it with our lives.

Men and women of the New Covenant have a singular advantage over those of the Old. We now know through Jesus that such communion with God is not limited to the temple. God is with us—always. He never leaves us. We do not need to enter his presence for we never leave it: his face is continually turned towards us. It is we who need to turn our faces towards his. When we do we shall not be disappointed. And like Martin Luther, we shall find in him all we need.

A WORD *from* JESUS

'I am the light of the world. Whoever follows me will never walk in darkness but will have the light of life' (John 8:12).

A PRAYER

Lord, bless me and watch over me.
Lord, make your face shine upon me
and be gracious to me.
Lord, look kindly on me and give me your peace.
Father, bless me;
Lord Jesus, bless me;
Holy Spirit, bless me.
And make me a blessing to others.

CELEBRATING *the* LAW

PSALM 119:1–8

Blessed are those whose way is blameless,
who walk in the law of the Lord!
Blessed are those who keep his testimonies,
who seek him with their whole heart,
who also do no wrong,
but walk in his ways!
Thou hast commanded thy precepts
to be kept diligently.
O that my ways may be steadfast
in keeping thy statutes!
Then I shall not be put to shame,
having my eyes fixed on all thy commandments.
I will praise thee with an upright heart,
when I learn thy righteous ordinances.
I will observe thy statutes;
O forsake me not utterly!

The PROMISE *of* BLESSING

Blessed are those whose way is blameless,
who walk in the law of the Lord.

A REFLECTION

Psalm 119 stands out not only as the longest psalm but also as the most emphatic celebration of the law of God. The frequent and sustained emphasis on law, commandment, word, ordinance, statute, precept, and judgment usually encourages the pilgrim through the psalter to give this one a miss! On the surface it speaks too much of effort from which the weary traveller recoils. But this carefully constructed poem merits serious attention and will surprise the attentive reader. What lies at the heart of this song is not a pious legalism that will secure God's favour. On the contrary, the poet is caught up in an intimately personal relationship with God and his devotion to God's law is a response to discovering that God loves him.

Commitment to the law does not secure the poet's relationship with God. Rather it is a responsive expression of a relationship that God himself has secured with his servant. The poet has no confidence in his own ability to keep the commandments unerringly. He longs to be perfect but he knows the realities of his own limitations. His ambition to live by God's law is a response to God's grace. There is, therefore, something surprisingly resonant of the New Testament here. Grace is the mother of devotion, not her daughter. Our commitment to God arises out of discovering that he has committed himself to us. Our love for God does not secure his love of us, but arises out of the love with which he first loves us. John spells this out: 'In this is love, not that we loved God but that he loved us and sent his Son to be the atoning sacrifice for our sins' (1 John 4:10). Throughout history God's love takes the initiative and reaches its climax in the giving of Jesus for us. This sacrifice draws from us the reaction of the beloved—love. The evidence of this love in our hearts is to be found in the actions of our lives. 'If you love me,' said Jesus, 'you will keep my commandments' (John 14:15).

When I was in parish ministry, I must have performed hundreds of weddings. Very often during the brief sermon which I would preach during the ceremony I would draw the attention of the bride and groom to the fact that the only words which they were obliged to say without repeating after me were 'I will'. In response to the question, 'Will you take... will you love, comfort, honour and protect...?' the answer comes without assistance: 'I will.' Those two words remind the couple of the nature of love. The will. I would point out that I did not enquire ,'Do you *feel* like taking...?' Feelings ebb and flow. What they felt for each other over a candle-lit dinner on their honeymoon would be very different from what they would feel for each other when the baby was crying every night for a whole year and they were arguing about whose turn it was to pace up and down the landing! If we go by our feelings solely then our relationships will be very stormy affairs. It is the will which is the bottom line of love. Whatever I feel, whatever is stacked against me, I *will* extend myself in favour of the other. Such is the nature of love. This is a hard enough lesson for us to learn in human relationships, but it is a lesson to be carried over into our relationship with God.

Our love for God, stirred by his for us, must be wilful. We cannot leave our relationship to the precarious rocks of feelings. If we love God, if we obey his commands only when we feel like it then we will be like a rudderless boat tossed about on the waters and driven by strong currents. The demonstration of our love will be found in our *wilful* attentions to his law.

When it comes to attending to God's law and commandments we are often short-sighted and legalistic. In our myopia we think that we ought to obey the law of God because this is the proper way to live and to live in this way will ensure a happier and healthier life. Indeed, that is exactly how most of us would read this promise of blessing. To be fair I don't think anyone could quibble much at that interpretation. But attending to the law of God is vital not because of its benefits so much as the fact that the law of the Lord is God's own disclosure of himself. The world 'law' (Torah) in this psalm denotes more than the Ten Commandments, more than the first five books of the Bible (the Pentateuch): it stands for *all* God's revelation of himself. God's character comes through in the commandments (human precepts revealing divine principles), in the prophets (God's word of judgment and mercy through his servant to his people), in the historical books of the scriptures (the story of God's engagement with the world) and through the Psalms (songs of worship prompted by the experience of his steadfast love). Here is the law of God. Yet it is not an end in itself but a means of grace. Not a means of securing God's grace, but the medium through which the grace of God is mediated to us. It is by wilfully attending to the law of God in response to his love that we saturate our personalities in the character of God. As we consciously walk with him through the scriptures so we begin to go at his pace, to tread in the same rhythm, to breathe in unison. Like two hikers we journey together, enjoying the same landscape. Like two lovers we delight in each other. May God save us from the short-sighted view of finding in the law of God only a set of rules for living. The scriptures themselves do not give us life.

The scriptures, the law of God, are the windows through which we see the one who alone can bless us with life eternal.

A WORD *from* JESUS

'You search the scriptures because you think that in them you have eternal life; and it is they that testify on my behalf' (John 5:39).

A PROMISE

I, N, take you, Jesus Christ
To be my Lord.
To have and to hold
From this day forward;
For better, for worse,
For richer, for poorer,
In sickness and in health,
To love, cherish and obey,
Till death and beyond
According to God's holy law;
And this is my solemn vow.

IMAGING GOD

PSALM 119:9–16

How can a young man keep his way pure?
By guarding it according to thy word.
With my whole heart I seek thee;
let me not wander from thy commandments!
I have laid up thy word in my heart,
that I might not sin against thee.
Blessed be thou, O Lord;
teach me thy statutes!
With my lips I declare
all the ordinances of thy mouth.
In the way of thy testimonies I delight
as much as in all riches.
I will meditate on thy precepts,
and fix my eyes on thy ways.
I will delight in thy statutes;
I will not forget thy word.

The PROMISE of BLESSING

Blessed are those who keep his commands:
and seek him with their whole heart (119:2).

A REFLECTION

'I have sought with my whole heart.'

Throughout the Bible there is a constant emphasis on seeking God, seeking his face, seeking his will. But how do we do this practically? Treasuring God's words in our heart, telling others what we have discovered of God, and meditating on his precepts are some of the practical suggestions that emerge.

This psalm from beginning to end is a practical way of seeking

God. Treasuring these words in our hearts and meditating on them are the means by which we, of our own free will, allow the love of God to impinge upon our consciousness. Biblical meditation is a particular art. It is different from other forms of meditation which empty the mind of all images in order to attain an inner stillness. Biblical meditation recognizes that the mind has a unique role in enabling humanity to be at one with the creator of the universe. Peace, *shalom*, welfare, and wholeness come to men and women not by rendering themselves and their minds empty and void of all images but by focusing and concentrating their minds on images of the one who ensures for us at-one-ment with himself. In tune with the creator who alone is the source of our welfare, we will then find peace and shalom.

Biblical meditation involves the mind exploring images of God. Meditation therefore involves the imagination; it is the exercise of making real to ourselves and present that which is remote or absent. A strong example of the power of imagination is the sexual fantasy. In our minds we can explore images so vividly that our sexual instinct is dramatically aroused. Even though we are not in the presence of the person, the imagination can make the absent body so present that our own body responds accordingly. The imagination possesses great force.

In our relationship with God we know theologically that he is omnipresent and with us always. We know that we do not actually enter his presence for, in truth, we never leave it. However, God is Spirit and intangible. We cannot touch him. He is not accessible to our physical senses—we cannot see, hear, touch, taste or smell him except in a metaphorical sense. We are bound by the limitations of our own physicality. Therefore, we, his spiritual and physical creatures, need to realize his presence, to make present the one who is physically inaccessible. We do this in the realm of the imagination. We focus our minds on the images of God in scripture, we explore the pictures, delight in the detail and so make present in our hearts the presence of God so that our whole being is stirred to love and devotion of the one who makes us and redeems us.

If you were to read through the whole of Psalm 119 you would find a galaxy of images that picture God and our relationship to him. Here are some of them:

Walking with God (v. 3)

Hiding his words like a treasure in your heart (v. 11)

Removing a veil from our eyes (v. 18)

Running the way of his commandments (v. 32)

Walking freely (v. 45)

Singing while you travel (v. 54)

Animal traps symbolize the obstacles to communion with God (v. 61)

Better than gold and silver (v. 72)

The hands of God making and fashioning you (v. 73)

Parched like a smoked wine-skin (v. 83)

The permanence of the earth symbolizes God's permanent faithfulness (v. 89)

God as teacher (v. 102)

God's word like a street light (v. 105)

God as shelter, as shield (v. 114)

God holds you safe (v. 117)

God's face shining on his servant (v. 135)

God's word pure and refined as in fire (v. 140)

God is 'physically' near (v. 151)

God as advocate in a lawsuit (v. 154)

God as a seeking shepherd (v. 176)

As you read each of these images your mind will most probably visualize each one. If you read them quickly it is possible that you register only an abstract idea. For example, 'God holds you safe' will register in your mind the idea of, say, protection. But if you dwell even briefly on these phrases your mind will involuntarily begin to picture a scene. This is the beginning of your imagination at work. What we do in meditation is to let the imagination explore the detail of the picture so that it becomes for us a parable of our relationship with God.

A WORD *from* JESUS

In the sermon on the mount Jesus appeals to our imaginations:

'Consider the lilies of the field, how they grow; they neither toil nor spin, yet I tell you, even Solomon in all his glory was not clothed like one of these. But if God so clothes the grass of the field, which is alive

today and tomorrow is thrown into the oven, will he not much more clothe you—you of little faith?' (Matthew 6:28–30)

A MEDITATION

I have gone astray like a sheep that is lost:
O seek your servant.

'Sheep', 'lost', 'gone astray' give us three points of information. They allow us to begin painting a picture.

In my mind I see an animal separated from the rest of the flock, hidden behind a hedge; I see this as a result of the sheep having been distracted and having pursued the distraction; I hear the animal bleating and sense the distress, loneliness and fear from being cut off; I sense the animal's panic. Although none of this is explicit in the verse it is not out of character with the petition that follows—'O seek'.

In my imagination I explore those occasions when I have felt lost and cut off from where I belong because of choosing to go off in another direction.

Returning to the scriptural image, I hear the one that is lost cry out, 'O seek your servant.' And already I am imagining a shepherd—hearing, caring, searching, rescuing. Although there is no explicit reference to a shepherd, his presence and rescue are implicit in the verse and this idea is consonant with the rest of the picture.

In my mind I willingly make the connection with the servant's prayer, 'O seek your servant.' The sheep cannot save itself, neither can the servant, nor can I. We are each of us dependent upon the rescue by another.

Now I make the prayer on my own: 'I have gone astray like a sheep that is lost: O seek your servant.' It is a prayer of confession and petition for salvation. I make it willingly.

I see a shepherd, the Good Shepherd, coming to me; seeking me. I imagine the meeting, the rescue, the relief, the joy. I wonder at the sheer goodness of God who is so committed to me and my welfare. Hallelujah! Praise begins to flow from my heart.

Everybody's imagination and meditation will be different. Different artists with the same paint, the same canvas, the same landscape, will, nevertheless, each paint a very different image. Each will be informed by the same objective data, but each personality has its own story of failure and need, of success and joy. Yet as we explore the images of God on the canvasses of our imagination, so we will observe the details that will evoke from the depths of our being a powerful response to God. On these imaginative canvasses we will seek God with all our heart.

THE LORD OUR KEEPER

PSALM 121:1—8

I will lift up mine eyes unto the hills:
from whence cometh my help.
My help cometh even from the Lord:
who hath made heaven and earth.
He will not suffer thy foot to be moved:
and he that keepeth thee will not sleep.
Behold, he that keepeth Israel:
shall neither slumber nor sleep.
The Lord himself is thy keeper:
the Lord is thy defence upon thy right hand;
So that the sun shall not burn thee by day:
neither the moon by night.
The Lord shall preserve thee from all evil:
yea, it is even he that shall keep thy soul.
The Lord shall preserve thy going out, and thy coming in:
from this time forth for evermore.

The PROMISE *of* BLESSING

The Lord shall preserve thy going out,
and thy coming in.

A REFLECTION

I remember once comforting one of my children after she awoke in the middle of the night. When I suggested saying a prayer as I tucked her up she dismissed the idea, telling me it would be no use at all because at this time of night Jesus would be fast asleep! As far as she was concerned, God was not available to her. That sense of absence often afflicts us throughout our adult life, leaving us feeling alone and lost. But this psalm gives us a reassuring picture of God who 'neither slumbers nor sleeps'.

The psalm opens with a question about where we shall find help. The answer reminds us that the one who is at our service is the originator of the universe. Such a truth that God is creator confronts us with God's power and God's purpose. The eyes of faith enable us to see that every situation is within God's mysterious purpose and no situation is beyond God's power to change. Yet the dominant theme is that of the Lord as the vigilant protector who will keep us from all evil.

The ultimate evil is to be separated from the love of God. Either as a temporary experience or as an eternal destiny this is the one evil from which we should pray to be delivered in the Lord's prayer. To be cut off and estranged from the source of life and love inevitably ends in lifelessness and lovelessness. Just as an astronaut swimming in space is lost into the eternal darkness when the line connecting him to the module is severed, so we, too, are in danger when alienated from the love of God. It is at this point that we realize again our utter dependence on God to keep us. Left to ourselves none of us would be safe.

All sorts of situations will arise that will cause us to stumble and fall. For Paul and the first followers of Jesus these were the 'tribulation, persecution, famine, nakedness, peril and sword'. For us as well there will be any number of situations, such as illness, accidents, depression, or unemployment that will make us doubt God's love for us. But however bad and tragic all these things are, when we are 'in Christ' they can never ever separate us from God. 'Neither death, nor life… nor things present, nor things to come, nor powers, nor heights, nor depth, nor anything else in all creation, will be able to separate us from the love of God in Christ Jesus our Lord (Romans 8:38–39). It is Christ the Lord who keeps us from the ultimate evil of being separated from God. However remote God may seem to us in our tragedies, Jesus Emmanuel declares that God is with us forever. He will never leave us. The ultimate evil is therefore vanquished.

A WORD *from* JESUS

'My sheep hear my voice. I know them, and they follow me. I give them eternal life, and they will never perish. No one will snatch them out of my hand' (John 10:27–28).

A PRAYER

Though the fig tree does not blossom,
and no fruit is on the vines;
though the produce of the olive fails
and the fields yield no food;
though the flock is cut off from the fold
and there is no herd in the stalls,
yet I will rejoice in the Lord,
I will exult in the God of my salvation. (Habakkuk 3:17–18)

The FAITHFUL PROVIDENCE *of* GOD

PSALM 127

Unless the Lord builds the house,
those who build it labour in vain.
Unless the Lord watches over the city,
the watchmen stays awake in vain.
It is in vain that you rise up early and go late to rest,
eating the bread of anxious toil;
for he gives to his beloved sleep.

Lo, sons are a heritage from the Lord,
the fruit of the womb a reward.
Like arrows in the hand of a warrior
are the sons of one's youth.
Happy is the man who has his quiver full of them!
he shall not be put to shame
when he speaks with his enemies in the gate.

The PROMISE *of* BLESSING

Blessed is the one who has his quiver full of them.

A REFLECTION

One Mothering Sunday our children gave my wife a card. It had a picture of screaming children driving their mother up the wall. The caption on the front read, 'When we're rude and naughty and you feel like pulling your hair out and climbing up the wall, just remember these two little words…' She opened the card and saw, 'Family Allowance!' (now Child Benefit). The consolation of parenthood being the little extra money it put in her purse each week!

In the Old Testament having children was the principal way parents provided for the social security of the family. The more children you had the greater your security as you grew older. Investing in a large family was their way of planning for their own future should they have an accident or become infirm through age. It was their form of protection, just like having 'a quiver full of arrows' against an enemy. In today's terms, a large family means both private and medical insurance and a pension plan! Times have changed. Responsible family planning has led to us making other provisions for our old age.

This psalm comes from the pen of someone who is acutely aware of the providence of God, conscious that every good gift comes from God. Like David in the book of Chronicles he celebrates God's material provision: 'Riches and honour come from you, and you rule over all' (1 Chronicles 29:12). There is nothing ascetic in this attitude. Jesus himself reminded us that the Father knows what our material needs are and will meet them accordingly.

To ignore this teaching about the faithful providence of God leads us to a lifestyle that is ultimately destructive. If we make ourselves the sole architects and builders without recourse to the designs of God we 'labour in vain'. Yet so often we make plans without laying them before God. Or, if we do bring them before the Lord we prescribe the solution to him without waiting upon him to direct us. We just want God to rubber-stamp our hasty decisions. The result of all this is feverish activity on our part. We go to bed late, we get up early. We burn the candle at both ends and we put a huge strain upon ourselves (depression, headaches, heart attacks); we put great pressure on our marriages (affairs, arguments, divorce); and we neglect our children (wrong relationships, drug and alcohol abuse, insecurity). We defend our behaviour by protesting that all this hard work was for the sake of the family: 'I was earning the money for you...' But the outcome has told another story. There is a poignant motto in the Book of Proverbs: 'Better is a dinner of vegetables where love is than a fatted ox and hatred with it' (Proverbs 15:17).

This psalm will serve us well if it makes us stop in our tracks and enquire of ourselves whether *all* our endeavours are God-centred or self-centred. 'Unless the Lord builds the house, we labour in vain.'

A PRAYER

Blessed are you, O Lord, the God of our ancestor Israel, for ever and ever. Yours, O Lord, are the greatness, the power, the glory, the victory, and the majesty; for all that is in the heavens and on the earth is yours; yours is the kingdom, O Lord, and you are exalted as head above all. Riches and honour come from you, and you rule over all. In your hand are power and might; and it is in your hand to make great and to give strength to all. And now, our God, we give thanks to you and praise your glorious name (1 Chronicles 29:10–13).

HARMONIOUS HOMES

PSALM 128:1–5

Blessed is everyone who fears the Lord:
and walks in the confine of his ways.
You will eat the fruit of your labours:
happy shall you be and all shall go well with you.
Your wife within your house:
shall be as a fruitful vine;
your children around your table:
like the shoots of the olive.
Behold thus shall the man be blessed:
who lives in the fear of the Lord.

May the Lord so bless you from Zion:
that you see Jerusalem in prosperity
all the days of your life.

The PROMISE *of* BLESSING

Blessed is everyone who fears the Lord:
and walks in the confine of his ways.

A REFLECTION

Here is a picture of domestic bliss. It is the Old Testament equivalent of the TV commercial for breakfast cereals! It is a psalm that plays into the hands of those who expounded prosperity teaching. This is the doctrine that if you seek God diligently you will find health and wealth.

There can be no doubt that to order your life on the principles of love and prudence will establish a more harmonious home than if you behave with unbridled selfishness. There is a truth therefore that obedience to the commandments of God leads to certain benefits. These are clearly recognized in the psalm. There can be little doubt, too, that a society made up of strong, healthy families will be a more decent nation than one where many are at risk through emotional turmoil and violence. But there is a world of difference between affirming the positive consequences of a life centred on God and actually *guaranteeing* health and wealth and a problem-free existence by obeying God's commandments. The experience of Jesus alone, not to mention the apostle Paul, was that obedience to the will of God often brought hardship and hostility. Nevertheless, the reality of evil and suffering in this life should not be allowed to detract from the central idea of this psalm that to order our affairs according to the character of God will produce certain harmonies in us and in our relationships that will be materially evident.

A husband is charged with loving his wife as Christ loves his Church. That is Good Friday love. It is in response to such sacrifice that a wife is expected to respect her husband. They are to be mutual servants (Ephesians 5:25, 33). Parents are warned against nagging. They must earn the respect of their children. Although the offspring are told to honour their parents it is not a slavish obedience to every parental whim. Parents can so easily abuse their power over their children. Mutual respect is called for here, too (Ephesians 6:1, 2). When it comes to the workplace, the employer is challenged to see that he is accountable to God for how he or she treats his or her employees and is forbidden to harass his or her workforce. This teaching was radical two thousand years ago and still is today. The person with power has a responsibility before God to *imagine* what it must be like for the other party and to act out of feeling for what it must be like to be in their shoes. That is compassion. This will lead to relationships of mutual respect and a healthier society.

The family features strongly in the psalm and one wonders what application this has for a society where divorce is so common. One of the most hurtful descriptions of a family affected by divorce is to call it 'a broken home'. Often the parent who has the care and control of the children is working doubly hard to ensure that the new home is happy and emotionally healthy. The Bible, in fact, does not specify the precise make-up of the family. People lived in households which were communities of the extended family and servants. In his letter to the Ephesians Paul spells out some of the principles of the relationships between husband and wife, children and parents, employers and servants (5:21—6:9). Mutual respect is the key to all communities which have Jesus Christ as their foundation.

A WORD *from* JESUS

Then his mother and his brothers came; and standing outside, they sent to him and called him. A crowd was sitting around him; and they said to him, 'Your mother and your brothers and sisters are outside, asking for you.' And he replied, 'Who are my mother and my brothers?' And looking at those who sat around him, he said, 'Here are my mother and my brothers! Whoever does the will of God is my brother and sister and mother' (Mark 3:31–35).

A PRAYER

Your will be done in me as it is in heaven. Amen.

EXERCISING FAITH

PSALM 129

Many a time from my youth upward
have they fought against me:
now may Israel say,
Many a time from my youth upward
have they fought against me:
but they have not prevailed.
They have scored my back as with a ploughshare:
they have opened long furrows.
But the Lord is righteous
and he has cut me free from the thongs of the wicked.
They shall be confounded and turned backward:
all those who hate Zion.
They shall be as the grass that grows upon the housetops:
which withers before it comes to any good,
with which no reaper may fill his hand:
nor the binder of sheaves his bosom.
And none who pass by shall say to them
'The blessing of the Lord be upon you:
we bless you in the name of the Lord.'

The PROMISE of BLESSING

And none who pass by shall say to them
'The blessing of the Lord be upon you:
we bless you in the name of the Lord.'

A REFLECTION

The greatest calamity in the world is to be denied the blessing of God, the Almighty. Whatever ambitions absorb our energies (and it is not wrong to set ourselves objectives and goals) the last verse of this psalm reminds us that to live without the blessing of God is a futile existence.

The testimony of the psalm is that the person committed to God and seeking his blessing always encounters obstacles along the way, not least from those who have no time for God. Frequently Christians interpret obstacles and opposition as signs that God does not want them to follow a particular path.

A friend of mine was trying to buy a flat. After the initial excitement of putting in an offer which was then accepted, her enthusiasm was deflated when she then had to face one problem after another. A Christian relative suggested to her that perhaps it was not after all the will of God for her to have this flat. The relative interpreted the difficulties as God saying 'no'. This sort of interpretation is common among Christians but has little basis in scripture and in the history of God's dealing with his people. If the people of God interpreted obstacles as God saying 'no' then Abraham would never have had any descendants, the children of Israel would never have entered the promised land, Solomon would never have built the temple, Jesus would not have died on the cross for our salvation, Paul would never have journeyed as a missionary, and the first Christians would have abandoned the causes of the Kingdom immediately when they encountered persecution. If scripture teaches any particular interpretation of obstacles and difficulties, it is that they are there to be overcome and not to be yielded to. My friend resisted the temptation to pull out, persevered and went on to enjoy the benefits of possessing her own home!

The danger of following the negative interpretation of obstacles is that it leaves the pilgrim in a terminal state of immaturity. We grow and mature only as we wrestle with the difficulties of life. If every time we face a problem we capitulate and retreat we never go forward into maturity. We never become aware of our inner strength; we never rely on God totally; we do not draw upon, and develop, our own resourcefulness; we pass up on the opportunity to sharpen our wits and increase our insight. It is not just our faith but our human potential that remains undeveloped. Just as muscles waste away if they are not exercised, so our personalities will never grow strong if we always retreat in the face of danger. Perhaps you face some awkward situation or relationship. Part of you, indeed, most of you, wishes that it would simply go away. But realistically there is no chance of that (in spite of your desperate prayers that God would remove the problem). Another option is that you plan to avoid the issue altogether. But an alternative way, a more biblical way, is to recognize that within the providence of God these obstacles are there for us to tackle and overcome. Our testimony will not only be, 'They have not prevailed' but also that 'he knows the way that I take; when he has tested me, I shall come out as gold' (Job 23:10). There is the testimony of a mature person.

A WORD *from* JESUS

Take heart from Jesus' encouragement:

> 'Blessed are you when men revile you and persecute you and utter all kinds of evil against you falsely on my account. Rejoice and be glad, for your reward is great in heaven, for in the same way they persecuted the prophets who were before you' (Matthew 5:11, 12).

A SPIRITUAL EXERCISE

Identify a problem or obstacle facing you (this may require some honest searching as we tend to push awkward things to the back of our minds and relegate them to the bottom of the in-tray). Describe the situation to God and in particular the goal that is being thwarted by the obstacle.

Examine the goal in the presence of God. How godly an ambition is it? If you are satisfied that the goal accords with God's goodness then in the awareness of God's presence plan a strategy for overcoming the obstacle.

Pray: 'Your will be done on earth as it is in heaven.'

ALWAYS
REJOICING

BLESSING GOD

PSALM 134

Come, bless the Lord, all you servants of the Lord,
who stand by night in the house of the Lord!
Lift up your hands to the holy place
and bless the Lord!

The PROMISE of BLESSING

May the Lord bless you from Zion,
he who made heaven and earth! (134:3)

A REFLECTION

Have you ever noticed what is missing from the Lord's Prayer? There is no note of gratitude. Jesus does not instruct us to say 'Thank you'. To order someone to show their appreciation robs the subsequent and forced expression of gratitude of all its meaning. God, with infinite patience, waits for us to express our gratitude of our own accord. He knows that it must come from us spontaneously. This psalm, however, gives us an example and encourages us to give thanks to adore God.

The Hebrew word for our blessing God is here exactly the same as the word for God blessing us. Our first thought might be to distinguish one from the other and to suggest that when people bless God it means 'to give thanks' and 'to adore', and that when God blesses his people it means, as we have seen in these psalms of blessing, gracing their lives with a range of material and spiritual benefits. But when God blesses people and people bless God they actually do the *same thing*, which is why in Hebrew it is here described by the same word (*baruk*). In this psalm to bless means to take delight in. Bless the Lord or delight in the Lord. May the Lord bless you or may the Lord delight in you. The word 'bless' suggests a relationship of mutual enjoyment. God delights in us: we delight in God. When God delights in us certain events, such as the absolution of sins, accompany that experience which we have come to call the blessings of God. When we delight in God certain events accompany that experience, such as thanksgiving. 'To bless' is 'to delight in'. 'Blessings' are those things which proceed from mutual delight: to be blessed by God is first and foremost to be delighted in by God.

The psalm calls our attention to the nature of the God who delights in us. He is the creator; the author of 'heaven and earth'. He is the source of blessing both spiritual and material. In the book of Revelation the Spirit discloses that God's plan for the universe involves 'a new heaven and a new earth'—a creation without flaws. The relationship of the people to God is compared with that of a bride adorned for her husband (Revelation 21). Here is a picture of mutual delight, and in the frame of that picture the intimate communion of mutual delight is spelled out: 'Behold the dwelling place of God is with his people. He will dwell with them and they shall be his people.' The ultimate blessing that flows from God's delight in us is that we should know him and therefore live for ever.

A WORD *from* JESUS

'Do you love me?' (John 21:16)

As he asked Peter after the resurrection, so, too, Jesus asks us this question every day.

A POEM

I gave myself to Love Divine,
And lo! My lot so changed is
That my Beloved One is mine
And I at last am surely His.

When that sweet Huntsman from above
First wounded me and left me prone,
Into the very arms of Love
My stricken soul forthwith was thrown.
Since then my life's no more my own

And all my lot so changed is
That my Beloved One is mine
And I at last am surely His.

The dart wherewith He wounded me
Was all embarbed round with love,
And thus my spirit came to be
One with its Maker, God above.
No love but this I need prove:
My life to God surrender'd is
And my Beloved One is mine
And I at last am surely His.

Teresa of Avila, 1515-1582
(translated by E. Allison Peers)

MATERIAL BLESSINGS

PSALM 144:1–7, 13–15

Blessed be the Lord, my rock,
who trains my hands for war,
and my fingers for battle;
my rock and my fortress,
my stronghold and my deliverer,
my shield and he in whom I take refuge,
who subdues the people under him.

O Lord, what is man that thou doest regard him,
or the son of man that thou dost think of him?
Man is like a breath,
his days are like a passing shadow.

Bow thy heavens, O Lord, and come down!
Touch the mountains that they smoke!
Flash forth the lightning and scatter them,
send out thy arrows and rout them!
Stretch forth thy hand from on high,
rescue me and deliver me from the many waters,
from the hand of aliens...
may our garners be full,
providing all manner of store,
may our sheep bring forth thousands
and ten thousands in our fields;
may our cattle be heavy with young,
suffering no mischance or failure in bearing;
may there be no cry of distress in our streets!
Happy the people to whom such blessings fall!
Happy the people whose God is the Lord!

The PROMISE of BLESSING

Happy are the people to whom such blessings fall!
Happy the people whose God is the Lord!

A REFLECTION

There is an earthiness about these psalms that unashamedly revels in the bounty of God's creation. The Christian Church and her doctrine have often been hijacked by a view of the world which sees the spiritual as good and the material as evil. This means we should shun material possessions because they are intrinsically evil and pursue the spiritual. Once people have put on these dark-tinted spectacles they read the Bible with prejudice. They latch on to all the passages that warn against the danger of money and materialism, using these texts as a means of berating everyone and reinforcing the sense of guilt in us whenever we begin to enjoy some material benefit.

It is true that Jesus speaks about money and possessions more than any other subject except for the Kingdom of God. It is true that the imbalance between the rich and the poor ought to make Christians examine their attitude to money, both personally and politically. It is true that there is an indulgence and hedonism that loses sight of the Creator that is unequivocally sinful. Yet against this emphasis we must stress a number of biblical points.

- The original goodness of God's creation. Remember that God saw all he had created and declared it 'very good'.

- The resurrection of the body of Jesus. This signals to us all that God's eternal plan for his originally good creation is material as well as spiritual.

- The Old Testament prophets. They were materialists in the best sense of the word. They cared about the material needs of the people. Religion wasn't to be a spiritual experience alone. It was to find its fullest expression in practical and material justice.

Of course, the *love* of money is a root evil and the rich must be careful of the seduction of self-sufficiency (1 Timothy 6:10, 17). But Paul reminds Timothy that it is God who richly furnishes us with everything to *enjoy*.

I can think of a person who appreciated expensive perfume, who knew a bottle of good wine, who enjoyed going to parties, who told a good story and was frequently entertained to meals. He was not only the life and soul of the party; he was the life and soul of the universe. His name was Jesus. He enjoyed creation. He enjoyed *his* creation. After all, 'all things have been created through him and for him' (Colossians 1:16). We in the developed world must not allow our understandable and proper sense of guilt about the inequity between the rich and the poor to rob us of the biblical vision that God has given us a material creation 'to enjoy'.

A WORD *from* JESUS

Jesus said, when you pray say,

'Father... give us this day our daily bread' (Matthew 6:9, 11).

A SPIRITUAL EXERCISE

Add up what you are worth financially.

Annual Salary:

Property less mortgage:

Savings less debts:

Contents of home:

Jewellery and clothes:

Car/bike:

Other:

Total

Thank God for the security and enjoyment these give you. Single out one thing that delights you out of the list. Let your mind dwell on this and enjoy what it means to you. Thank God that in his grace *he* has given these to you to *enjoy*. Thank God for his open-handed generosity to you.

> Pray: 'Father, bless me with the same generous spirit
> that I may share joyfully and freely
> all that you have given to me.'

Unrestrained Praise

Psalm 146:1–10

Praise the Lord.
Praise the Lord, O my soul:
while I live I will praise the Lord;
while I have any being:
I will sing praises to my God.

Put not your trust in princes:
nor in the sons of men who cannot save.
For when their breath goes from them
they return again to the earth:
and on that day all their thoughts perish.

Blessed is the man whose help is the God of Jacob:
whose hope is in the Lord his God,
the God who made heaven and earth:
the sea and all that is in them,
who keeps faith for ever:
who deals justice to those that are oppressed.
The Lord gives food to the hungry:
and sets the captives free.

The Lord gives sight to the blind:
the Lord lifts up those that are bowed down.
The Lord loves the righteous:
the Lord cares for the stranger in the land.
He upholds the widow and the fatherless:
as for the way of the wicked he turns it upside down.
The Lord shall be king for ever:
your God, O Zion, shall reign through all generations
Praise the Lord.

The PROMISE of BLESSING

Blessed is the man whose help is the God of Jacob,
whose hope is in the Lord his God.

A REFLECTION

This is the first of the five concluding psalms of the psalter (the traditional name given to this book of the Bible) that begin with 'Hallelujah'. The inspiration of this unrestrained praise is the character of God who is the same today as he was yesterday and will be forever. The God of Jacob is the God of Jesus. The prelude to reliance on God and to the experience of his faithfulness is a disappointment and disillusionment with people in authority. To be thwarted by people with power is deeply frustrating: you have no way of getting them to change their minds, no leverage to force them to give you a chance to prove yourself. There is no court of appeal. A natural human response is to exchange intimidation for resentment. David had the right attitude. Firstly, he remembered that they are only people who bleed and die like the rest of us (it was Churchill who coped with his nerves when speaking in the House of Commons by imagining his audience sitting in their underwear!) Secondly, David drove himself to a new reliance upon God. That is a good example to follow. As David drew upon God, there were specific aspects of his character that inspired him to praise and worship.

Jacob's God

Jacob was no saint but he, too, came to the point of throwing himself on God. He wrestled with the angel of God and vowed, 'I will not let you go, unless you bless me' and God did bless him. We could do with that same tenacity.

God the creator

Whoever doubts the power of God should in their imagination stand at the ocean's edge and contemplate the vast energy of the seas. It is God who generates the power of the sea.

God the faithful

It was Hudson Taylor, the great missionary in China, who learned that the secret of faith was the personal discovery of the *Lord's* faithfulness to us.

God of justice

God is pledged by the character of his own being to right the wrongs in the world. Establishing God's Kingdom on earth is about changing social structures as well as individual hearts.

The Lord of freedom, sight and healing

Here for all to witness is a picture of an interventionist God. He doesn't sit back in some remote paradise untouched and uninvolved in the hurt of his creation. He is committed to restoring his flawed creation.

A WORD *from* JESUS

At the beginning of his ministry, Jesus said:

> *'The Spirit of the Lord is upon me,*
> *because he has anointed me to bring good news to the poor.*
> *He has sent me to proclaim release to the captives*
> *and recovery of sight to the blind,*
> *to let the oppressed go free,*
> *to proclaim the year of the Lord's favour' (Luke 4:18, 19).*

A PRAYER

> *Holy Spirit*
> *make me just as Jesus*
> *and as just as Jesus. Amen*

DESPAIR & HOPE

IN THE DARKNESS

PSALM 22:1–2

My God, my God, why have you forsaken me:
why are you so far from helping me,
and from the words of my groaning?
My God, I cry to you by day but you do not answer:
and by night also I take no rest.

A REFLECTION

We come now to Psalm 22, which gives voice to those times when God and his blessings feel remote. We all know the long dark night of the soul. It is an experience which Jesus himself endured, the sense of being abandoned by God.

Jesus spoke the opening line of this psalm from the cross. It is a psalm of fluctuating moods. Despair and hope. To what extent the whole psalm was in the mind of Jesus we can never know. But from the earliest time it was seen as a prophetic commentary on the passion of Jesus. It offers us a powerful demonstration of the way the Old Testament was fulfilled in the New. We can take a few verses at a time and reflect on them so that they become to us like a wall of stained glass or like stations of the cross that draw us into and interpret to us the death and resurrection of Jesus Christ.

In this psalm, and especially in Jesus quoting from it, we find permission to express our own sorrows and doubts. There is no attempt to bottle up the emotions. Full and free expression is given to the fearful loneliness that grips the soul of the person who suffers. God seems distant and silent. It is the experience of Job who goes forward and back, turns to the right and to the left and feels that God is not there (Job 23). The soul-baring of Job, of the writers of the psalms, and of Jesus himself has freed us and given us permission to be honest with God and with ourselves about our fears and sense of desolation.

The opening verses of this psalm, although born out of tragedy, strike us with a paradox: on the one hand they speak of desertion, distance and silence; on the other hand they speak of an intimate, tenacious, and personal relationship with God. The psalmist cries of being 'forsaken' and of God being 'so far' away and not 'answering' his pleas for help. Yet this has to be contrasted with the psalmist's intimate and personal communion with God ('My God, my God') and with his tenacious relationship ('by day... and by night'). Here is the paradox: it is in the moment of desolation that the sufferer binds himself fastly to God. This stark contrast reminds me of the paradox to be found in the prayer of the prodigal son as he returns home. 'Father... I am no longer worthy to be called your son' (Luke 15:19). If he really believed that to be the case he would not have called him 'Father'! Yet, in spite of his selfishness and wilful rebellion, and in spite of what he said, the son knew that he was still his father's son. In the same way, the psalmist knew that in spite of the catastrophes surrounding him, God was still 'my God'. And that is how he reached out to him. In an even greater and more mysterious way Jesus knew that, in spite of being the Lamb of God and absorbing all the painful wrongdoing of the human family, nothing could in the end destroy the intimate Father–Son relationship he had with God.

During my time in parish ministry people often came to me confessing a sense of abandonment by God. Their worry was that this feeling meant that they no longer had a relationship with God, that they had lost their faith. After they told me their story I would point out to them that the very act of coming to talk with me was indicative of faith. If they had no faith at all then the last person they would go to would be a priest or a minister. Coming to me was their way of holding on to God. That's faith. And faith enough for God. Your reading of this book may place you in the same category. Your decision to read it is an attempt to hold on to God because at this moment so many things seem to conspire against you believing in God. Yet somehow you are here on this page and in these words, 'My God, my God'. But these are not just words on a page, they rise up from within the depths of your own heart. You are saying them to God: you are speaking to God. It may be dark and cold in the cell where you live, it may be painful and exposed on the cross where you hang, but the agonizing cry, 'My

God, my God, why have you forsaken me?' shows that you have more faith than you realize. Otherwise, you would not have ventured as far as this sentence.

A WORD *from* JESUS

'Who touched my clothes?... Your faith has made you well; go in peace' (Mark 5:30, 34).

Faith here is simply and literally holding on to Jesus. This is faith enough for God.

A SPIRITUAL EXERCISE

In your imagination follow the example of the woman who touched the tunic of Jesus. Imagine a step further. Jesus holds out his hand to lift you up. Take hold of his hand. Now physically tighten the grip of your hand so that the fist is now clenched. Feel the strength of your grip.

That is the measure of the strength of your faith. Thank God that he has inspired such faith in your heart.

GOD WITH US

PSALM 22:3–5

But you continue holy:
you that are the praise of Israel.
In you our fathers trusted:
they trusted and you delivered them;
to you they cried and they were saved:
they put their trust in you
and were not confounded.

A REFLECTION

These verses hold together both the transcendence and the immanence of God. On the one hand, he is 'holy', remote and distant,
transcending all that he has created. On the other hand, he is present with his people, especially in those events when he has
'saved' and 'delivered' them. God is always and constantly both
transcendent ('holy') and immanent ('Emmanuel: God with us').
It is our perception and experience of him which varies.

There are occasions when we will be all too aware of God's
detachment and independence of all he has made. There will be
times when we would love God to be more accessible, even to be
visible and tangible. 'If only we could see him, touch him, then
we'd really believe.' The fact that he is spirit and not physical
emphasizes the gulf between us. God is over and above us. On
other occasions we will be aware of his presence with us. These
moments will often take us by surprise. In a time of loneliness
our heart fills up with a sense that God loves us; in a period of
confusion our mind is flooded with peace, sensing that there is a
purpose at work in and through the chaos; in a moment of darkness a placid joy mingles with our tears as an unexpected light
pierces the gloom, inspiring us to persevere. These experiences are
intimations that God is with us. His spirit invades our personal

world and inspires in us love, peace and joy. These are some of his acts of deliverance and salvation.

So God is both intimate and distant. This paradox encourages us to know that even though God is the creator and sustainer of the universe we can know him in a personal relationship; but then again even though we may know him personally we can never limit him to the boundaries of our own experience.

This paradox is captured for us in the opening line of the Lord's Prayer. This prayer is so familiar that we lose sight of how extraordinary the opening words must have been to the disciples. 'Our Father, hallowed be your name.' Here are two completely and mutually foreign ideas. 'Father' speaks of a family and intimate relationship. 'Hallowed' speaks of awesome reverence of the holy. The latter idea was more in keeping with the disciples' approach to God: the chasm of sin constantly reminded them of the need to offer sacrifices so as to bridge the gulf between them and a holy God. Such was their reverence that they would never speak nor even write his name. Although they knew that God was the Father of Israel none of them would dream of addressing him in such an intimate way as 'Abba' ('dear Father'). Then comes Jesus. They hear him praying: he enjoys an intimate relationship with God and always calls God 'Father'. Such is the quality of his praying that they ask him to teach them how to pray. The answer was startling: 'Say "Father" .' But how could those who so hallowed the name of God be so familiar with him as to address him in such an intimate way? It is the cross that makes such a contradiction possible.

The only time that Jesus never addresses God as 'Father' is when he is on the cross and quoting from this psalm. In this moment of absorbing the wrong-doing and wrong-being of humanity, the Lamb of God takes away the sin of the world. Sin comes between God the Father and God the Son. The Son is as fatherless as the Father is sonless. In that cry from the cross it is as if Jesus is denying himself the right to call God 'Father' so that we who, on account of our sin, have no right, might be able to say when we pray, 'Father'. Certainly it is through the death of Jesus that we are reconciled to God (2 Corinthians 5:17ff), and because of this we are now sons and daughters of God in whom the Spirit urges us to pray, 'Abba, Father' (Galatians 4:4–7). It is the cross that harmonizes our experience of the transcendence and the immanence of God. The over-and-above-us God is the now-and-forever-at-one-with-us God. He has always been with us. As Paul reminded the philosophers of Athens, 'He is not far from each one of us. For "in him we live and move and have our being"' (Acts 17:27, 28). It is the cross that enables those seeking him and reaching out for him to break through into that other dimension and to find him. The hallowed one is our Father.

A Word *from* Jesus

Jesus said:

> 'Those who love me will keep my word, and my Father will love them, and we will come to them and make our home with them' (John 14:23).

A Prayer

Father, Father, Holy Father,
Father, Father, Righteous Father,
In your holiness you stand apart from our sin.
In your righteousness you made him to be sin
who knew no sin.
So that we may be clothed with his righteousness.

My mind is humbled by such knowledge.
My heart is awed by such mystery,
My soul is alive to know that you
are at one with me and I with you.

Father, dear Father, good and kind
Give me this day the bread I need,
Forgive me as I learn to forgive those who hurt me,
Protect me from the powers of darkness.

In your glorious and hallowed majesty
Rule the world with justice and mercy
So that your will might be done
on earth as it is done in heaven.

Yours is the kingdom—you rule over the world.
Yours is the power—the power of creation
and the power of Resurrection.
Yours is the glory—in heaven and on earth.

PRAYER *as* COMMUNION

PSALM 22:6–8

But as for me I am a worm and no man:
the scorn of men and despised by the people.
All those that see me laugh me to scorn:
they shoot out their lips at me and wag their head, saying,
'He trusted in the Lord, let him deliver him:
let him deliver him if he delights in him.'

A REFLECTION

I remember walking home with one of my daughters one night. She was on the pavement, I on the road. 'Get off the road, Daddy,' she urged me. I assured her it was quite safe as I knew there were no cars coming. Realizing her pleas were getting her nowhere she began, tongue in cheek, to pray aloud: 'Dear God, please make Daddy get off the road.' Just to show her that intercessory prayer does sometimes 'work' I duly obliged and joined her on the pavement! There was glee on her face as she raised her hands and proclaimed, 'You see, I've got *magic*!'

Many adults have not outgrown this child-eye's view of prayer. We would love to have such power. Many Christians go in search of the right 'formula' of faith, the special words and rituals so that they can, in effect, cast their 'spell' and work 'magic'. The difference between the Christian faith and the occult is that in the latter the practitioners seek to manipulate the supernatural power whereas in the former the people of faith *submit themselves to the will of God*. This submission in faith leads to communion which is the essence of prayer. Prayer is not the manipulating of supernatural power so that you can get your own way. It is abiding in Christ and Christ abiding in us. It is communion with God, aligning our will with his will. When that happens perfectly *then* you can ask whatever you will and of course it will happen (see Jesus' words in John 15:7).

I remember as a young man asking God on one occasion to provide three different things. Within a short space of time each of the three things happened as I had prayed. My joy was tempered with unease. It felt like magic. What worried me was that I had doubts about my own judgment. What would happen if I asked God for something which proved eventually to be bad for me? Would he give it to me? I hoped not! As my Christian understanding developed, I came to see that the prayer I had made on that occasion happily accorded with God's will for me. Either because I was in tune with God or by accident I had sought from God what God decided in that moment to give me. Since that time there have been countless occasions when I have sought all sorts of things that have not happened and I am glad, although I was often bitterly disappointed at the time.

The central line of the Lord's Prayer 'Your will be done on earth as it is in heaven' was echoed by Jesus in the Garden of Gethsemane when, having besought the Father to whom all things are possible to remove from him the cup of suffering, he prayed, 'Yet not what I want, but what you want' (Mark 14:36). Perhaps in the Garden Jesus could imagine both his supporters and his enemies shouting at God as they saw him on the cross: 'He trusted in the Lord, let him deliver him.' It seemed a perfectly reasonable prayer. 'Dear Lord, he's such a good person, please help him.' We have all prayed similar prayers—sometimes in faith, sometimes in anger. So much is at stake: we want the onlooker to see God at work doing something spectacular to confound all the sceptics. How we wish we could pray for and secure the miraculous healing of a good friend. Then everybody would believe (and so would we, at last without doubt). But when the prayer is not answered in the way we had asked we imagine the shaking heads and scornful laughter of those who have no faith in God. We begin to shake our heads and scorn our own faith. The disbelief of unbelievers undermines our own belief.

But if we want to grow in faith and in the school of prayer we have but one example and inspiration. If Jesus, in all his goodness, sought to do the will of his Father as the foundation of his communion with him, so ought we. Regardless of the outcome.

A Word *from* Jesus

'Now my soul is troubled. And what should I say—"Father, save me from this hour"? No, it is for this reason that I have come to this hour. Father, glorify your name' (John 12:27).

A Spiritual Exercise

In these words of Jesus we have two possible prayers with which we can approach God in every situation; either 'save me' or 'glorify your name'. Our first and natural reaction to new situations is 'save me'. Jesus, our example, chose the latter: 'glorify your name'. Either on paper or in your mind lay before God the situations you find yourself in today. Think especially of the situations from which you wish to be saved. Consciously commit each one and yourself to God with the prayer, 'Glorify your name.'

GROWING THROUGH CRISIS

PSALM 22:9–11

But you are he that took me out of the womb:
that brought me to lie at peace on my mother's breast.
On you have I been cast since my birth:
you are my God even from my mother's womb.
O go not from me for trouble is hard at hand:
and there is none to help.

A REFLECTION

It is the complete lack of fantasy in the gospels that is so compelling. Jesus is no 'superman'. On the contrary, he is a man who cries, gets tired, and needs to sleep, eat, and drink like the rest of us. He has the supernatural power to do miracles. But he is always restrained. There is nothing grandiose or exaggerated about his gestures. The recording of the miracles in the gospels is remarkably understated. None of the evangelists goes into very great detail. And when the miracles do cause a stir Jesus seems to play them down. For example, he swears Jairus and his wife to silence after he raises their daughter from her death-bed (Luke 8:56); and when he has fed the thousands with loaves and a few fish and raised their expectations of him he then promptly sends them all away (Mark 8:10); and when one day they come to force his hand and make him their king he escapes such a high profile and disappears.

There is nothing in the gospels of the swashbuckling antics of a hero from the realm of fantasy. Jesus may well be the Son of God but his ordinary humanity fills every page. His conception may have been different but he came like us all 'from my mother's womb'. And after the trauma of childbirth he found 'peace on my mother's breast'. And although he was endowed with the supernatural power of God he experienced throughout his life that 'trouble is hard at hand'. Through these human experiences Jesus grew and developed like the rest of the human family.

Life for us all consists of a series of 'crises'—puberty, adulthood, marriage, bereavement. The developing personality is confronted by new situations and has to adjust. This is the path of maturity. Luke tells us that 'Jesus increased in wisdom and in years' (2:52). The word he uses to describe Jesus' behaviour originally meant 'making your way forward by chopping away obstacles'. That is how we all mature. Jesus had to contend with the emotional and physical changes of puberty; he had to work at the changing relationship with his parents as does every young adult, moving away from dependency to mutual respect; he had to come to terms with his own sexuality. To deny all this would be to cast him in a mould of being less than human. Jesus encountered the full range of human experience and through them he, too, matured as a person. He wasn't born with the brain and emotions of a thirty-year-old. He matured to this point.

Jesus knew the pain of loss and grief. When John his cousin died (Matthew 14), Jesus lost not just a relative but a soulmate who understood his mission in a way that few others did and a co-worker who paved the way for his ministry. This loss led Jesus like many of us to 'withdraw privately to a solitary place'. The loss creates inner turmoil because the fixed points go and we feel cut adrift from our moorings. Whether that loss is through death, divorce, retirement or moving away, it is a time of emotional adjustment. These are the experiences which fashion us. Were they foreign to Jesus? Not at all.

As Jesus hangs on the cross he looks down upon his own mother, from whose womb and upon whose breast he drew human life. Dying son and grieving mother. But she can do nothing 'and there is none to help'. Jesus is alone. The ultimate human experience of death is one which we all have to undergo alone. And although at the scene there are those who expect the Son of God to perform like some fantastic 'superman' and jump down from the cross, he who has the power of creation at his fingertips endures obediently to the end. There is no escape from death for Jesus. His only escape, as it is for every human being, is through death.

A WORD *from* JESUS

It was out of Jesus' own experience of friendship and loss, of bereavement and grief that, on the cross…

> When Jesus saw his mother and the disciple whom he loved standing beside her, he said to his mother, 'Woman, here is your son.' Then he said to the disciple, 'Here is your mother.' And from that hour the disciple took her into his own home (John 19:26–27).

A PRAYER

Consider in your imagination the moment of your own death.

> 'Yea, though I walk through the valley of the shadow of death,
> I will fear no evil:
> for thou art with me' (Psalm 23:4).

Jesus, who has passed through this way, will be with us by his Spirit and will lead us out of the valley of the dying into the world of the truly alive.

PERMISSION *for* FEAR

PSALM 22:12–13

Many oxen surround me:
fat bulls of Bashan close me in on every side.
They gape with their mouths at me:
like lions that roar and rend.

A REFLECTION

The land around Jordan was famous for its strong cattle. The bulls of Bashan were frightening creatures. A herd of these bulls closing in on you was a fate worse than death. This picture—this nightmare—stands in this psalm as an image of the fear of destruction. To what an extent Jesus himself was gripped by such a fear we can never know, for no soul is transparent to others. And yet there are episodes in his life when Jesus shows his feeling of fear. In John 12 he says with candour, 'My soul is troubled. And what should I say—"Father, save me from this hour"?' The fear is again expressed in the Garden of Gethsemane in the sweat like drops of blood. Here Jesus confesses frankly his distress and sorrow. It is important for us to learn from this example that there is no shame and no sin in confessing our fears. It is more healthy to express and confront our fears. It is more healthy to express and confront our fears than to repress and stifle them under a blanket of so-called faith.

My youngest daughter when she was two got very frightened on Guy Fawkes night. She loved the sparklers and enjoyed standing behind the window watching the Roman candles and Catherine wheels. I had asked for fireworks without bangs. Unfortunately, the next few I lit all went off with large bangs! Tabitha was terrified and ran away from the window; nothing and no one could persuade her to come to the window again. The following day she came across the burnt-out cases in the garden. She came into the house, called for me, took me by the hand, and together we

inspected the burnt-out fireworks. 'Bang, bang,' she said defiant-
ly as she prodded and recalled the terror of the previous night.
Entirely off her own bat she went back into the kitchen and
returned with a plastic bag and together we picked up the old
fireworks. When the bag was full of all these things which had
frightened her, she took to the dustbin and, with a confidence
beyond her years, threw it in the bin. I marvelled at the way this
little person was handling and coming to terms with something
that had frightened her.

In this child's behaviour there seemed a lesson for many adults
whose lives are paralysed by fear. To acknowledge and confront a
fear is more healthy than to hide it. Of course, the presence of her
father enabled Tabitha to find the confidence to handle the fearful
objects. Similarly when chronic fears grip people a counsellor,
friend or therapist may play an important part in enabling the person to face the fear. Yet, whether the fear is great or small, it is for
us to see in this psalm and in the example of Jesus *permission* for
us to talk about what frightens us. It is not lacking in faith for us
to acknowledge our fears.

A WORD *from* JESUS

Jesus began to be sorrowful and troubled. Then he said to them:

'I am deeply grieved, even to death' (Mark 14:34).

A SPIRITUAL EXERCISE

Identify a source of fear. Recall an incident when this fear affected
you. In your imagination re-live the incident, conscious that Jesus
is with you. Tell him the source of your fear.

THIRSTY *for* the WATER *of* LIFE

PSALM 22:14–16

I am poured out like water and all my bones are out of joint:
my heart within my breast is like melting wax.
My mouth is dried up like a potsherd:
and my tongue clings to my gums.
My hands and my feet are withered:
and you lay me in the dust of death.

A REFLECTION

Although so much of the gospel is taken up with the passion of Jesus it is remarkable that there is so little attention to the physical and violent details of crucifixion. We are given the basic facts, the cross, the nails, the thirst, the last breath, the spear, the blood and the water. By today's standard of reporting, however, these aspects are understated. The lack of hyperbole again reinforces my own belief in the historicity of the gospel accounts. The full horror of the crucifixion is left to our imaginations.

The poetic images of this psalm stir us to think what it must have been like for Jesus to hang, nailed to a cross in the midday sun. His death, prolonged and agonizing, culminated in asphyxiation with the ribcage collapsing on the lungs. The physical pain was excruciating, 'the mouth dried up like a potsherd: the tongue clinging to the gums'. So from the cross Jesus cries out, 'I thirst'. His need was a double one. The sheer thirst to moisten his lips, his tongue, his mouth, which the taste of coarse wine would only partly and cruelly quench, and the spiritual thirst to be at one with his Father whose nearness is contorted as the Son, Lamb-like, takes to himself the sins of the world. How Jesus must have sung that other song within his soul: 'My soul thirsts for you the living

God. When shall I go and meet with God?' His thirst is both a physical and a spiritual need.

John is the only evangelist to record these words from the cross: 'I thirst.' Poignantly it is he of all the four who projects the image of thirst so prominently in the teaching of Jesus both in his gospel and in the Book of Revelation. 'Whoever drinks the water I will give him will never thirst again. Indeed, the water I give him will become in him a spring of water welling up to eternal life' (John 4:13–14). One of the many ironies of the Gospel of John is that the one who promises that those who come to him shall never thirst again is himself found thirsting in the extreme. As he bears our sins on the cross, estranged from the Father, he thirsts for that close communion which he has enjoyed from before the world began. And, because he has once and for all taken away the sins of the world, we who thirst to know God can now be satisfied. Through this thirsting our thirst is quenched.

'It is done!' say the Alpha and the Omega in the Book of Revelation. 'I am the beginning and the end. To the thirsty I will give water as a gift from the spring of the water of life' (Revelation 21:6). The Spirit and the Bride repeat the invitation: 'Come… let everyone who is thirsty come. Let anyone who wishes take the water of life as a gift' (Revelation 22:17). The one who is 'poured out like water' (Psalm 22) is the Fountain where all who drink will live now and for ever.

A WORD *from* JESUS

Then he took the cup, gave thanks, and offered it to them, saying, 'Drink from it, all of you. This is my blood of the covenant, which is poured out for many for the forgiveness of sins' (Matthew 26:27–28).

A SPIRITUAL EXERCISE

Place in front of you a glass of cold water. Imagine the day is hot. Your mouth is dry. You have not drunk for some time. Allow your imagination time to evoke the feelings of being thirsty. Now reach for the glass and sip the water. Hear these words of Jesus: 'Whoever believes in me will never be thirsty' (John 6:35). Drink all the water. Take time to thank God for his promise to quench your thirst.

NAKED

PSALM 22:17–19

For many dogs are come about me:
and a band of evildoers hem me in.
I can count all my bones:
they stand staring and gazing upon me.
They part my garments among them:
and cast lots for my clothing.

A REFLECTION

Here is the ultimate humiliation. Even before you are dead they are disposing of your possessions. It is a cruel picture. John tells us that Jesus suffered the same indignity when the soldiers divided up his clothes and then cast lots for the seamless undergarment (John 19:23). There is a tendency for most of us to read these episodes with an air of superiority and to think that we would never have done such a thing. We group all those who had a part in Jesus' death as 'them' and confidently see ourselves as part of the small faithful band of followers who stayed with Jesus to the end. We would never dream of saying it out loud but inwardly we thank God that we are not like those who hounded Jesus to the cross.

We read the passion narrative and shudder as we hear the crowd clamouring for his death. 'Here is your king,' shouts Pilate and the mob screams for his blood, the blood of Christ, 'Away with him! Away with him! Crucify him!' (John 19:15). In this appalling incident we stumble on a disconcerting truth: Pilate asks, 'Shall I crucify your King?' Quietly, inwardly we distance ourselves from the crowd as we whisper in our souls, 'no'. It is 'them' who want him dead, not us. It is 'them' with their hard faces and callous souls who thirst after the blood of the Saviour of the World, not us. It is 'them' who shout 'crucify', not us.

But here is the sad and sorrowful truth. Here is a truth that deals a blow to our pride and self-righteousness. When Pilate enquires 'Shall I crucify your King?' it is *we* who must also with 'them' shout, 'Yes. Crucify him!' For, if he does not go to Calvary and to the cross how shall *we* find a Saviour to die in our place and to cleanse us from our sin? It is with a heavy heart that we, too, must join the crowd and add our voices to those who press Pilate to send Jesus to the cross. We need a Saviour as much as 'them'. And so we join the chorus: 'Away with him! Take him away! Crucify him!' Gone is the air of superiority. We are in the dust, clamouring for his death, casting lots for his garments, driving nails through his body, hoisting him on a wooden cross, and marvelling at his grace, 'Father, forgive them'.

A WORD *from* JESUS

'Father, forgive them; for they do not know what they are doing.' And they cast lots to divide his clothing (Luke 23:34).

We crucified Jesus, but he prays for us to be forgiven.

A PRAYER

'Shall I crucify your king?'
Forgive me, Lord.
'Shall I crucify your king?'
Have mercy, Lord.
'Shall I crucify your king?'
Yes, Lord.
'Shall I crucify your king?'
Yes, take him away.
'Shall I crucify your king?'
Take him away and crucify him.
He is crucified.
Forgive me, Lord.
Have mercy, Lord.

The Father forgives you.

Take the clothes.
They're yours.
Your inheritance.
A sign.
All that is mine is yours.
Life eternal.
Mine.
Now yours.

The LIBERATOR

PSALM 22:20–22

O Lord do not stand far off:
you are my helper, hasten to my aid.
Deliver my body from the sword:
my life from the power of the dogs;
O save me from the lion's mouth:
and my afflicted soul from the horns of wild oxen.

A REFLECTION

The one person that could have saved Jesus from the fate of the cross was Pontius Pilate. 'Do you not know that I have power to release you?' Pilate chides Jesus (John 19:10). The irony of this question is that it is in reality Jesus who has the power to set Pilate free. It is Pilate who is in chains as the events of the passion demonstrate. He is cornered and compromised by the powerful factions who play on his own insecurities. He thinks he is a free man but he is manacled. On the other hand, Jesus who stands on trial bound and browbeaten is the only one truly free person in the whole scenario. He has come into the world to liberate those who are slaves to sin and chained in darkness, including Pilate himself. If only Pilate could have seen it!

When we make this psalm our own prayer and ask God to hasten to our aid and deliver us from oppression, we are placing our lives in the hands of the unique liberator. The one who bandages our wounds has himself been wounded, who anoints our bruises has himself been bruised, who dabs the tears in our eyes has himself shed his own tears, who strengthens us in our times of oppression has himself felt the power of the oppressor, who sets us free has himself been bound, who comforts us as we die has himself stared into the face of death.

God has committed himself to a ministry of liberation. It is beautifully captured for us in the book of Revelation: 'They will be his people, and God himself will be with them; he will wipe every tear from their eyes. Death will be no more; mourning and crying and pain will be no more, for the first things have passed away' (Revelation 21:3–4).

Who is it that wipes away the tears? God himself. Yet again our servant—the deacon God, ministering to us. There is something very gentle and delicate about wiping away the tears from someone's eyes; it is a poignant image: the gentleness of God, who in Jesus has cried his own tears, sensitively attending to our own tear-stained faces. The meekness of God complementing the majesty of God.

A WORD *from* JESUS

'I am gentle and humble in heart, and you will find rest for your souls' (Matthew 11:29).

A PRAYER

Just as I am, though tossed about
with many a conflict, many a doubt,
Fightings within, and fears without,
O Lamb of God, I come.

Charlotte Elliott, 1789–1871

STIRRINGS *of* HOPE

PSALM 22:23–25

I will tell of your name to my brethren:
in the midst of the congregation will I praise you.
O praise the Lord all you that fear him:
hold him in honour O seed of Jacob
and let the seed of Israel stand in awe of him.
For he has not despised nor abhorred
the poor man in this misery:
nor did he hide his face from him
but heard him when he cried.

A REFLECTION

The key changes from minor to major here. In the midst of the trauma and tragedy there draws a fresh awareness of the character and purposes of God. The circumstances have not changed. Yet the poet has sensed that God is there, that God has heard him, that God is with him, that God is here, now. The awareness inspires a new confidence and a song of praise. This is a genuinely spiritual experience that transcends the material circumstances. It is akin to that experience of Paul who, out of all his difficulties, could confidently write: 'And we know that in all things God works for the good of those who love him, who have been called according to his purpose.'

These moments of spiritual awareness cannot be forced; they simply come upon you and are instances of spiritual perception. When my children were much younger, they enjoyed looking at those picture-cards which could be seen in two different ways: one looked like a candlestick, but when you looked again it changed into the profile of two faces, nose to nose; another looked like the head of an old woman but when you looked again it was the face of a young woman; and yet another looked like footprints in the snow but when you looked again it was the face of Jesus. I remember the first time I saw this last picture-card and being told to see in it the face of Jesus. I looked and stared but could not see it. The harder I tried the more elusive it became. Then some time later I glanced casually at the card and there it was as clear as light, the face of Christ. How could I have failed to see it? Nothing in the picture had changed—the contours were the same—but now I could see. In a similar way, we can stare at the circumstances of our life and read them in one way, perhaps being pessimistic and desperate. Then we look again and are surprised to discover, in exactly the same canvas, hope instead of despair, light instead of darkness, joy instead of sadness. There is no accounting for the change in perception. At least, nothing of the circumstances has changed and induced a different attitude. It is just that now we see it all from a different angle. Faith is a matter of seeing life from a different angle and interpreting the contours of events in a different light. That is supremely what Jesus was able to do not only in his words from the cross but in the upper room when he celebrated the Passover feast with his disciples.

On one level the master and his followers were enjoying a meal together. On another level they were celebrating the glorious deliverance of God's people. And, on yet another level, they were eating the body of Christ and drinking the 'blood of the new covenant, poured out for many for the forgiveness of sins'. Whether the disciples saw this and to what extent they understood it at that moment is unclear. I suspect that they saw but didn't perceive, heard but didn't understand. But then one day they did.

The question that troubles every believer is how can we ensure these moments of revelation. Now we know from the scriptures what things stifle these moments of truthful disclosure, such as pride and hardness of heart, although even these are not insurmountable obstacles to the power of God as the conversion of Saul dramatically demonstrated. We know, too, from the scriptures that humility and openness to God are fertile ground for the sowing of the seed of faith. But in the end we have to conclude that those moments of spiritual awareness are not deeds of discovery but gracious acts of revelation. In other words, the moment of spiritual insight is something that is *given*, not something that we *achieve*. Revelation is essentially different from discovery. Revelation is that which God does, discovery is what we do.

Revelation is a grace of God, discovery is a human work. Revelation is a gift, discovery is a deed.

This is an uncomfortable truth on two grounds. First, in a world orientated towards achievement it is a frustration that we cannot achieve the spiritual dimension in the way that we are taught to in the material realm. The same values do not apply. Second, in the writing and reading of such books as these there can be no guarantee that there will be any liberating, soul-enlarging spiritual insights. We may put much effort into discovering the character and purpose of God—and such effort is commendable, cultivating the ground for the seed of faith—but the moment of revelation, when God discloses the truth about himself, is a matter which he himself decides and determines. Paul reminded the Corinthians:

> *What no eye has seen,*
> *nor ear heard,*
> *nor the human heart conceived,*
> *what God has prepared for those who love him—*
> *these things God has revealed to us through the Spirit*
> *(1 Corinthians 2:9–10).*

Theology is a matter of revelation. Any Christian who studies the scriptures, any theologian who attempts to systematize doctrine and fails to grasp this issue is doomed to blindness. Our trust in God includes trusting him to reveal himself to us, his character and his purposes.

When we receive holy communion, what we experience of God in this celebration of the Lord's death will be determined by God himself. The act of divine grace is not only the death of Christ but also the moment of revelation and understanding that leads us to see in the tragic death of a good man the salvation of the world.

A WORD *from* JESUS

Let us remember the words of Jesus:

> *'I am the living bread that came down from heaven. Whoever eats of this bread will live for ever; and the bread that I will give for the life of the world is my flesh' (John 6:51).*

In your imagination reach out empty hands to receive the sacrament of bread and wine. Hear Jesus say as you take the bread in your hand: 'This is my flesh for the life of the world.' Hear Jesus say as you take the cup in your hand: 'My blood of the covenant for the forgiveness of sins.' Wait in silence on God, holding the sacrament.

Now, eat and drink in remembrance that he died for you and feed on him in your heart by faith with thanksgiving.

TRUE SACRIFICE

PSALM 22:26–27

From you springs my praise in the great congregation:
I will pay my vows in the sight of all that fear you;
the meek shall eat of the sacrifice and be satisfied:
and those who seek the Lord shall praise him,
may their hearts rejoice for ever!

A REFLECTION

The meek shall eat of the sacrifice and be satisfied

It is the understanding of Christ's death as a sacrifice for the sin of the world that transforms Bad Friday into the most excellent day in the history of the human family. That Friday is Good because on the cross of Calvary Jesus endures our hostility, absorbs the pain of our wrongdoing and intercedes for our forgiveness. It is the sacrificial Lamb of God, taking away the sins of the world, who blesses that day and turns it into Good Friday.

The idea of 'sacrifice' has fallen on hard times. People are understandably reticent to speak of God as some giant deity who demands the blood of sacrifice so as to assuage his anger. So when it comes to describing the work of Christ on the cross people drop the word 'propitiation' in preference to 'expiation'. The former suggests satisfying God's wrath, the latter reflects the idea of flushing away the offensive stains. The God of Jesus Christ is not, of course, a bloodthirsty pagan deity who lusts after sacrifice. And yet he is the God of justice and mercy who sets himself against injustice and oppression in all its individualistic and social expressions. He is the just and merciful God who *requires* the removal of the offence of evil and sin from his creation. That is his character and his purpose in sending his son Jesus into the world.

When Jesus hangs on the cross and takes to himself the sins of the whole world it is certainly an expiation of our offences, a washing away of all our unrighteousness. But it is more than that. Because it is God himself who *requires* the remission of our sins, there is after all an element of propitiation. It is not just that we need cleansing but that God requires such in order for us to be free from sin and therefore free to commune with him. There is both a horizontal and a vertical dimension to the cross. The horizontal line acknowledges our need to find someone, nobler than ourselves, to expiate the sins that wreck our communion with God and over which we have no power. The vertical line signals that in his merciful justice it is God who requires that someone undefiled by sin remove and remit the sins that separate us from God. What is remarkable is that it is God himself who makes that sacrifice, and that he had this in mind even before the foundation of the world (see 1 Peter 1:18–20).

The cross is both expiation and propitiation, addressing human need and expressing divine necessity, the character of God. When we feed on this sacrifice we *shall* be satisfied, for to feed on the risen, crucified Lord is to be nourished by God himself.

A WORD *from* JESUS

When Jesus had received the wine, he said, 'It is finished.' Then he bowed his head and gave up his spirit (John 19:30).

Jesus, both High Priest and Victim, offers the ultimate sacrifice of his very self. It is done. Expiation and propitiation. We are free because of his death.

A PRAYER

Holy Father,
you reel back in righteous anger at the desecration
of our lives.
Holy Father,
you lean forward in mercy, giving yourself
in love and forgiveness.
We worship you.

Glory to God in the highest,
and peace to his people on earth.
Lord God, heavenly King,

almighty God and Father,
we worship you, we give you thanks,
we praise you for your glory.
Lord Jesus Christ, only Son of the Father,
Lord God, Lamb of God,
you take away the sins of the world:
have mercy on us:
you are seated at the right hand of the Father:
receive our prayer.
For you alone are the Holy One,
you alone are the Lord
you alone are the most High,
Jesus Christ, with the Holy Spirit,
in the glory of God the Father. Amen.

The GRACE *of* GOD

PSALM 22:28–29

Let all the ends of the earth remember
and turn to the Lord:
and let all the families of the nations
worship before him.
For the kingdom is the Lord's:
and he shall be ruler over the nations.

A REFLECTION

An international student was doing post-graduate studies in the city where I worked at one time as a minister of the gospel. She was brought up a Buddhist and was highly intelligent and well educated. She found the time in England difficult, as do many international students, but found friends in several of the churches in the city. Through them she began coming to church and out of this started to call upon Jesus to help her. To her surprise she found that he answered her simple prayers and dispelled the pessimism that haunted her. I met her after the first occasion when she came forward to receive communion. There were tears in her eyes and wonderment on her face. She could not get over the fact that all of us, men and women, young and old, rich and poor, black and white, had all drunk from the same cup. This was unheard of in her culture. She discovered that at the Lord's table and in his kingdom there is no such person as an untouchable. Nobody is beyond his grace. The invitation into his kingdom extends to all classes, all races, all nations:

Let all the ends of the earth remember
and turn to the Lord:
and let all the families of the nations
worship before him.

Although both Jews and Christians have failed down the ages to show it consistently, the God of Abraham and of our Lord Jesus Christ is a God without frontiers. It is because he loved the whole world that he sent his only son Jesus Christ so that whoever believes in him, regardless of background, should not die but have everlasting life.

The grace of God has always burst the banks of human prejudice. If you had asked the average self-respecting religious person in Jerusalem about the eternal destiny of the thief on the cross he would have left you in little doubt as to his future. The man utters the name of Jesus. He asks Jesus not to forget him when he gets into the Kingdom of Heaven. I don't suppose the thief knew much theology—I doubt if he had an inkling of the classical theories of atonement. His prayer is blunt, desperate and to the point, 'Jesus, remember me.' The response from Jesus is embracing, 'I tell you the truth, today you will be with me in paradise.' The promise of heaven. Not for the pious, not for the good, not for the theologian, not for the priest, not for the minister. But for the one who just cried out for Jesus.

'Jesus, remember me when you come into your kingdom.'

A WORD *from* JESUS

He replied, 'Truly I tell you, today you will be with me in Paradise' (Luke 23:43).

A PRAYER

Throughout today on the hour make the thief's prayer your own: 'Jesus, remember me when you come into your kingdom.' (There is a beautiful Taizé chant that may help you enter into this prayer.)

LIVING *as* PEOPLE *of the* BLESSING

PSALM 22:30—32

How can those who sleep in the earth do him homage:
or those that descend to the dust bow before him?
But he has saved my life for himself:
and my posterity shall serve him.
This shall be told of my Lord to a future generation:
and his righteousness declared to a people yet unborn
that he has done it.

A REFLECTION

This song which began in darkest sorrow ends gloriously on a note of triumph and praise. The poet's progress through the psalm is a parable of the life of every individual and community, of the people of god and of Christ himself.

In the same way, we can reflect on how the resurrection of Jesus signals the end of all misery, especially the ignominy of Good Friday which was surely one of the bleakest days in the history of the human family. 'But,' as a black preacher once intoned, 'that was Friday—and Sunday's comin'!' The contrast between Good Friday and Easter Sunday could not be greater. On Friday, the disciples were dejected and disillusioned, 'But that was Friday—and Sunday's comin'!' On Friday, the authorities thought that they had everything under control. 'But that was Friday—and Sunday's comin'!'

The physical, tangible, bodily resurrection of Jesus was an explosion of power and light in a world of darkness and despair: death had been defeated and the sway of evil terminally undermined. In raising Jesus from the dead, God acted decisively against death and the ravages of sin. He did this not as some subjective, spiritual and psychological exercise in the individual minds of those favourably disposed to Jesus. He did it publicly, objectively, historically, physically in the material world that demonstrated in its very fabric the consequences of evil, sin and death.

Let me put it this way. If you find weeds in the garden destroying the flowers you do not deal with the problems by soothing your soul with beautiful music. This may provide psychological and spiritual relief but it does not address the destruction. Instead, you enter the garden to challenge and destroy the enemy. We can see around us the real and physical and material manifestations of evil and sin: these are not illusions but are physically real. They occur in the material world that God has made and in which, in spite of the flaws, God continues to delight. In the physical resurrection of Jesus, God deals decisively with the consequence of evil in the *physical* as well as the *metaphysical* realm. He enters the material world to challenge and destroy the enemy. He raises Jesus from the dead and death is devoured. 'Death has been swallowed up in victory.' He acts against the destructive weeds and gives life to the garden.

What the physical resurrection of Jesus also declares is that God has a continuing plan for his creation, physical as well as spiritual. The resurrected body of Jesus shows to the world that God has a purpose beyond death for the material dimension of life. If the resurrection of Jesus had been only a psychological or spiritual experience we could conclude with errant believers that all God was really interested in was the soul and that therefore you don't really need to give priority, and do justice, to the material needs of people. But the prophets of the Old Testament, the teaching of the New Testament, the resurrection of Jesus all tell another story and deliver a different message.

A WORD *from* PAUL

For I handed on to you as of first importance what I in turn had received: that Christ died for our sins in accordance with the scriptures, and that he was buried, and that he was raised on the third day in accordance with the scriptures, and that he appeared to Cephas, then to the twelve. Then he appeared to more than five hundred brothers and sisters at one time, most of whom are still alive, though some have died. Then he appeared to James, then to all the apostles. Last of all, as to someone untimely born, he appeared also to me…

If Christ has not been raised, then our proclamation has been in vain and your faith has been in vain. We are even found to be misrepresenting God, because we testified of God that he raised Christ— whom he did not raise if it is true that the dead are not raised. For if the dead are not raised, then Christ has not been raised. If Christ has not been raised, your faith is futile and you are still in your sins… If for this life only we have hoped in Christ, we are of all people most to be pitied…

When this perishable body puts on imperishability, and this mortal body puts on immortality, then the saying that is written will be fulfilled: 'Death has been swallowed up in victory.'

'Where, O death, is your victory?

Where, O death, is your sting?'

The sting of death is sin, and the power of sin is the law. But thanks be to God, who gives us the victory through our Lord Jesus Christ.

Therefore, my beloved, be steadfast, immovable, always excelling in the work of the Lord, because you know that in the Lord your labour is not in vain. (1 Corinthians 15:3–8, 14–17, 19, 54–58)

HYMN *of* PRAISE

Hail thee, Festival Day! Blest day that art hallowed for ever.
Day wherein Christ arose, breaking the kingdom of death.
Jesus has harrowed hell; he has led captivity captive:
Darkness and chaos and death flee from the face of light.
Hail thee, Festival Day! Blest day that art hallowed for ever.
Day wherein Christ arose, breaking the kingdom of death.

Sixth-century hymn